DID YOU SURVIVE THE WAR?

Dedicated to my wife Audrey (1921-1990)

DID YOU SURVIVE THE WAR?

C W 'JERRY' JARROLD
(with Ken Delve)

Raydon Wings Ltd
and
Aviation History Centre

First Published in 2006 by
Raydon Wings Ltd
Raydon
Suffolk
www.raydonwings.co.uk
In association with
Aviation History Centre
www.aviationhistorycentre.com

British Library Cataloguing-in-Publication Data
A catalogue record for this book is available from the British Library.

ISBN 0 9552 2960 X

Design: Luke Delve, Andrew Delve, Aviation Editorial Services

Printed and bound in Great Britain by Biddles Ltd, King's Lynn, Norfolk

Contents

Introduction   4

Early Days   6

Into the Royal Air Force   9

Flying Training   14

First Tour – No. 80 Squadron   23

Rest Period – No.13 Operational Training Unit   69

Second Tour – No.181 Squadron   73

Remembering the Past   98

Epilogue, May 2005   107

Appendices:
    A. Record of Service   109

    B. Aerodromes Landed At   111

    C. Aircraft Flown   112

    D. Letters from Colleagues   112

    E. The Death of Fg Off Harry Horsey   116

PREFACE

When I was approached to help Jerry with this book it seemed an ideal opportunity to help relate the story of one of the many hundreds of 'ordinary fighter pilots' – not aces, not highly decorated, not known by the public - but the backbone of the vast majority of combat ops flown by the RAF in World War Two. These 'ordinary' pilots came from diverse backgrounds, undertook the RAF's grueling and unforgiving, not to say dangerous, 'laying on of hands' to become aircrew, and went into action with trepidation, determination, courage and that belief that all young men, and especially fighter pilots, have of invulnerability; best not to think about what might happen, just get on with the job and take it a day at a time.

During my 30 years of aviation research and writing, and my 20 years as RAF aircrew, I have met a great many 'old boys', aircrew and groundcrew from World War Two, and one aspect has always been evident – the matter-of-fact way in which they recall their flying careers. To them it seemed nothing special: they made friends, lost friends, drank a great deal, had what the uninitiated would think was a strange sense of humour, and did the best job they could for their mates, their Squadron, the RAF and their Country, usually in that order.

Jerry's book is full of matter-of-fact understatement, such as the almost daily Cab Rank missions with the Typhoons of 181 Squadron in the early months of 1945: how can you truly grasp the change from the peaceful scenario of cruising around waiting for a target to the dive into the invariably heavy and accurate flak, looking for the target, lining up and firing the Rockets – no chance to dodge the flak – pulling out and leaving the danger zone; did everyone make it? How about following a *Tiffie* that takes a direct hit from flak and barrels into the ground? Do that twice a day knowing that you've got to keep doing it until you don't come back, you get posted for a rest tour or the war ends. So much for the matter-of-fact lists of missions flown!

With combat ops on Hurricanes, Spitfires and Typhoons from North Africa, into Southern Italy, over Normandy on D-Day and into NW Europe, Jerry's story covers some of the RAF's major operational areas. The mess burning down at Bu Amud after his 21ˢᵗ birthday celebration, the shooting-down of his colleague by the Royal Navy minesweeper they were escorting, the visit of the RAF dentist with his Arab-powered bicycle drill; these and many more 'ordinary' events provide an insight into life with 80 Squadron in North Africa. Borrowing a Tiger Moth to give a 'joy ride' to a relative, visiting – at very low level – an Aunt's cottage … and avoiding the accusation of low-flying that followed, add a personal perspective to the endless round of escort missions flown by 80 Squadron Spitfires from bases in Southern England.

Like so many pilots the end of the war brought an end to Jerry's flying career with the RAF and he was soon back in civvies. It was sixty years later that he took to the air again, reliving for a brief moment those early flights as a U/T pilot on Tiger Moths. In his twilight years this 'ordinary' fighter pilot thought back to a different era, a time when men and women served in that life and death struggle that was World War Two.

Memories of faces and events, tragic events and comical interludes lie side by side in this typical tale of an ordinary fighter pilot.

Ken Delve, Swaffham, December 2005

DID YOU SURVIVE THE WAR?

INTRODUCTION

My story depicting almost six years service in the Royal Air Force during World War Two really began to take shape towards the end of my life, rather than at the beginning.

With my very good friends, Jean and Roy Cane, we were celebrating Roy's birthday in early October 1997 with an enjoyable meal, and whilst taking coffee in the lounge of the local restaurant, we were discussing a recent air show at nearby Duxford Airfield. There, the largest gathering of Spitfires since the war years had been on show. John and Priscilla Anderson, who were, by chance, also taking coffee after their meal, overheard us chatting.

John said he couldn't help being interested in our conversation and decided to intervene (against the efforts of Priscilla to restrain him). We chatted and exchanged addresses, and he also invited us to be his guests at Raydon Air Show the following year. He organised and ran the Show from his nearby home. A couple of days later I received a very nice letter and invitation to visit him for a natter. For the last seven years I have visited John and Priscilla at their lovely home next to the former World War Two USAAF airfield at Raydon in Suffolk. John has one of the largest private collections of aviation books I have ever seen and on my visits he loans me a dozen or so books from this superb collection. On a number of occasions he has suggested I write down my experiences with the possible objective of producing a book.

My dear wife Audrey sadly passed away some 15 years ago in 1990, and it was she who always kept me going with memories, and indeed was the prime mover in keeping much of the memorabilia - log books, maps, small black-and-white photographs of the wartime days, and other items - in a safe place. This also included preserving my old uniform. By and large I personally did nothing, except perhaps show keenness in reading and collecting a fair number of World War Two flying books.

My two friends Jean and Roy have been great pals since my wife died, and helped me through those terrible dark days after her untimely death. Jean was always very interested in my wartime RAF experiences, especially as she was, for quite a time before her retirement, working in the RAF Library in London, and both Jean and Roy have tried to encourage me to write my story. This included me joining an organisation called The Typhoon and Tempest Association, which met every June at the old RAF Shoreham airfield.

The organisation is run by Ken Rimell and I have attended for the last few years. It was at one of these Reunions that I noticed a distinguished white-haired gentleman, whom I seemed to recognise as our Wing Commander Flying, No.124 Wing, 2nd TAF (Tactical Air Force). I served with 181 Squadron as part of this Wing at B86 (Helmond) in Holland in early March 1945. Shortly after I joined the Squadron, Wing Commander `Kit' North-Lewis DSO, DFC and Bar was shot down - 24th March 1945 on the Rhine Crossing Operation. He evaded capture and returned safely a number of days later. I walked over to him and introduced myself as one of his Typhoon pilots and asked how he was, and we had quite a long chat. His first words to me, after the usual pleasantries were, "…and, did you survive the war?" - followed almost immediately by "of course you did, otherwise you wouldn't be here!" Hence the title of this book! So after much hesitation I decided to start to put pen to paper on 1st September 2002.

C W 'Jerry' Jarrold ex Fg Off RAFVR
80 and 181 squadrons RAF

EARLY DAYS

I remember very little of my early days at my birthplace, Ilford, but have just fleeting memories of living in a fairly large house in Forest Gate, East London, owned by my Aunt and Uncle. My father I only saw on rare occasions as for almost all of his working life he was away at sea serving as a Merchant Navy Engineer. Father served in both World Wars, latterly as a Chief Engineer. Following early retirement in 1948 he died aged 58.

I suppose my first memory was starting school in 1927, and a few other memories such as being taken to the local Post Office (in Forest Gate) to open up a Post Office Savings Account with a very small deposit. Certain aspects of the house I can recall, but the most memorable was the time I spent at the end of quite a long garden, watching the steam trains passing on four tracks to and from Liverpool Street Station and on to East Anglia. I remember spending hours trying to identify the very many slow and fast trains speeding by, just below, down an embankment. Eventually we all moved into a larger house, again owned by my Aunt and Uncle, in Hainault Road in Leytonstone; still in East London. Here at the still tender age of 7 or 8 years I joined a new school called Oxford & Elsom House; a small private school, where I stayed until I left in 1937 at the age of 15.

Our house was rather large with six bedrooms and four reception rooms, a billiard room, a fine large attached conservatory with quite a large fishpond, and rockery nearby. There was a long well kept garden, at the end of which was a large garage with a workshop with two rooms above. The garage was connected by a very large pair of sliding gates, which opened up to a service lane at the back of the property. My Uncle kept his lovely large Austin car in the garage, and in 1934 he allowed a dozen or so of my school friends to occupy the two upper rooms. Here we planned to form and operate a model aeroplane club, and so we knocked the adjoining wall down to form one large area with a number of work benches to accommodate 14 or 15 places for the building of model balsa wood aeroplanes. Thus started our great interest in flying, and aeroplanes and the RAF in particular.

These few years were very happy and busy, and there was always someone turning up every evening and at weekends. We organised many visits to model aeroplane factories and meetings, plus other air events, including at least two visits to the annual RAF Hendon Air Display. At the Hendon displays it was the antics of the bi-plane fighters that appealed and not the lumbering bombers – no doubt like many young lads my first real spark of desire to become a fighter pilot. Eventually in 1939, mainly because of the approach of the war and the fact that a number of us had left school, (as I did in 1938, to seek a job in the outside world), the club closed.

Of the modellers, Ken Robinson, Dennis 'Tubby' Porter and I tried to keep in touch for a while. The three of us eventually became RAF pilots and we all survived the War. I met up with 'Tubby' Porter after the War and we went about together with another friend from 181 Squadron days, Syd Ainsley, but I never saw Ken Robinson again. He stayed in the RAF and was serving in the Far East as a Liberator Captain when he fell ill from some obscure tropical disease and was shipped home to the RAF Hospital well after the war ended. I learnt all this from his wife, who he had married a few years earlier. She wrote to tell me about Ken and that he had sadly died in the RAF Hospital from this rare tropical disease. She also told me that his mother and father (who I knew well from our school days) had, at the outbreak of war, moved to Devon. The day before Ken died they were travelling up from Devon to see their son in hospital when they were both killed in a car accident. With Ken being an only child, it now meant the whole family was wiped out in just a couple of days: all so very sad.

'Tubby' Porter became a Wellington pilot, but because he was two or three years younger than me, he apparently never made it onto an operational squadron. After

'Tubby' and I were demobbed in 1946 we spent a lot of time together at the weekends, and he introduced me to a pub in Epping Forest - the Wake Arms - and it was there in early 1946 that I met my future wife, Audrey, the daughter of the licensee, Mr. Norman Bulmer. Another RAF friend, Syd Ainsley, who lived in Rugby would spend many weekends with me, and the three of us would go to Wembley Ice Hockey matches and also to see Leyton Orient football team play. Audrey's father would also join us on our visits to see 'The Orient'. I was beginning to see more and more of Audrey and visits from 'Tubby' and Syd became less frequent. 'Tubby' eventually married a girl from Scotland. Audrey and I attended the wedding, and later, Tubby together with his wife, and friend Syd, attended our wedding in 1952.

After that 'Tubby' and I failed to keep in touch. He later became a director of Hill Samuel and was based in South Africa for many years. We did meet up some years later when we lived at Potters Bar, Hertfordshire but we never met again and I believe he has now passed on.

INTO THE ROYAL AIR FORCE

Soon after I left school in 1937 1 joined a medium-sized company in Finsbury Square, London EC2. The Head Office and main warehouse of this multiple grocery company operated some 100 stores mainly around London and the Home Counties, and were also tea and coffee blenders, and importers. I was taken on as a Junior Buyer in the General Grocery Buying Office, which included a Chief Buyer, Director, two other Buyers, plus a small clerical staff and myself.

I worked for 2½ years there before presenting myself at a RAF Recruiting Office on 7th March 1940 (my 18th birthday) with the object of being selected to train as a Pilot. Details were taken and I was sent back to await a call to attend an Aircrew Receiving Wing. It was over a three-month wait, but on 26th June 1940 I reported to RAF Cardington in Bedfordshire, the Aircrew Receiving Wing, where I underwent the various medical tests and interviews, and it was with much horror that I was informed I was medically unfit for aircrew, but that I could volunteer to become a Wireless Operator. Feeling very dejected I accepted the offer of becoming a Wireless Operator (Ground) and again returned home to await a posting for an induction course. I was to report to RAF Bridgenorth, which we all described as a "bull centre". It was here that we were kitted out and were subjected to a three-week drill course, which was very hard work, but we certainly knew how to march and drill! Again, I was sent home to await further posting, as I was now an eager AC2 (Aircraftman 2nd Class).

I shall always remember the day I had to report to RAF Cardington - for my father was on one of his rare visits home, and he and my mother saw me off at London St. Pancras Station for my train to Bedford, nearest station to Cardington. I wasn't to see my father again until late in 1944 – at Christmas time, when he happened to be home for a short spell between the North Atlantic voyages. He made crossings to and from

North America, Canada, and sometimes South America. I well remember his advice to a very young lad joining up with all those other young men, telling me not to get carried away with the wrong types. All very vague, but of course, he meant well!

My next posting was to RAF Pembroke Dock in South Wales, a Sunderland Flying Boat Station. I seemed to be attached to 210 Squadron (Sunderland) in the Armoury Section as an AC2 'dogsbody' - somewhere to keep me quiet whilst waiting for my Wireless Operation Course! This period was to last from the 22nd of July 1940 to the 11th of January 1941. It was the beginning of the Battle of Britain, and South Wales seemed, and was, many miles away from the action. Just on the other side of the bay was a huge oil refinery at a place called Neyland, and the German bombers had set fire to many of the oil tanks; indeed, parts seemed to be on fire the whole time I was there. Almost every other night a single German bomber flew over and dropped a few more bombs on the fires to keep them going, and again it seemed months before the huge fires were finally put out or brought under control.

The work in the Armoury was quite interesting, and one of the jobs was to go out into the bay in a flat bottom boat to the various Sunderland flying boats at anchor in the bay either to de-bomb or bomb-up with what seemed to be quite small bombs, which we had to man-handle to and from the bomb-catches under the wings. I was never able to get a ride in a Sunderland - mainly because they were either going or coming back from very long patrols. In bad weather de-bombing could be a bit fraught, especially with the boat going up and down with the wind and the waves. As a bomb was released from its housing under the wing of the flying boat, a number of us had to take the weight of the bomb on our shoulders, but with movement of the boat and the Sunderland, many was the time that the bomb fell with a clang to the bottom of the boat (metal floor). Never heard of any going off! Whilst at Pembroke Dock I was able to enjoy two periods of leave at home in Wanstead, Essex before our small house was damaged by bombs, and my mother moved out to stay near one of her sisters at Pangbourne, Berkshire.

The only trouble with going home on leave was the very long and tiresome railway journey. Part of the journey meant night travel with many stops or hold-ups mainly through enemy bombing action; especially at Milford Haven and in the Bristol area. Sometimes the journey took approximately 24 hours and included stops at Bristol, Newport, Swansea, Llanelli, and Carmarthen, and the trains were usually packed solid with service men. Horrible journeys!

On 11th January 1941 I was suddenly posted to RAF Yatesbury for a month's intensive course on how to operate the new radar systems. At that stage we had never heard of radar and we were all sworn to secrecy. We worked on night and day shifts operating the radar screens and it all seemed to be a very hit or miss affair, but, nevertheless, at the end of the course, we were all promoted to LAC (Leading Aircraftmen) and awarded the Wireless Operator sleeve badge.

On the 14th of February 1941, I and one other LAC were posted, even further away from all the action, to RAF Radar Station Castlerock, near Londonderry, Northern Ireland. I well remember boarding a corridor train with the other fellow at Belfast Station bound for Londonderry. Even at that period in time (1941) during the journey, there were a number of men (civilians) running along the train corridors and engaging in fighting with other gangs of men. When we asked some of the passengers what was going on, they said "Oh it's always like this - they are Protestants and Roman Catholics - they are always fighting each other"! Times don't change much!

Castlerock was set in beautiful countryside by the sea - quite near a place called the Giant's Causeway - and the other fellow and I were billeted in a small stone cottage for sleeping, with one bedroom and one quite small bed for two airmen (I just couldn't believe it!). There was a wash basin in the bedroom, with two water jugs, and hot water was only supplied early in the morning by the landlady for shaving and washing, with no sign of a bathroom! When I asked about the toilet, she said 'that's the little hut at the bottom of the garden', with a plank over a small running brook.

A very long way to go to at night, so we made sure we always had a torch handy.

The radar screens were in a largish wooden hut with accompanying sets of aerials, and we worked in shifts of so many hours over each 24 hours. It was very long boring work with simply no action, except the occasional false alarm caused by friendly aircraft not identifying themselves. There was also a very large amount of shipping just off Londonderry, as convoys used to form up there for the North Atlantic crossing. I was at Castlerock for almost three months, but I never got used to the outside loo, nor the jugs of hot and cold water for washing and shaving. However, there was one small bit of joy, for nearby was a very good golf course called Castlerock (or Coleraine) Golf Course, and thanks to the generosity of the club members, the RAF were allowed to use the course whenever we wanted to. They even supplied us with bags of clubs and balls! Being my first experience, I thoroughly enjoyed my introduction to the fine game of golf.

One day in May 1941 my Commanding Officer (CO) handed me a communication from, I believe, the Air Ministry. It said, in effect, that there had been a mistake in my medical assessment, and that I was, in fact, medically fit to be considered for Pilot Training, and if I so desired I could apply to re-muster as a Pilot U/T (Under Training). I was, of course, delighted by the news and accepted immediately. On the 19th of May 1941 I was scheduled to report to the Aircrew Reception Wing at Stratford-upon-Avon. This meant more medical tests and more interviews, this time by quite an interesting board of senior officers overseen by a Group Captain. When I was asked about my education, I believe I impressed them. I said at school I had some difficulty with mathematics, although algebra was one of my favourite subjects. However, in order to get myself ready for Pilot Training before joining, two of my friends and I had decided to go in for a correspondence course. I chose maths and trigonometry and worked hard to get a good set of marks. They seemed very impressed and said that I would be recommended for Pilot Training and, as an experienced airman (LAC Wireless Operator - Radar), I could lead and encourage the more junior members of the course I would be posted to. They all wished me good luck, which was most surprising!

So, after a few days leave at home (I don't think my mother was overjoyed at me becoming a pilot, but she was kind enough to encourage me) I was posted on the 25th of May 1941 to Cambridge ITW (Initial Training Wing). The squad I was in consisted of some 25 to 30 young men, and we were housed in one of the famous colleges, Magdalene, where we slept, ate and studied as if we were actual university students. We marched in squads to various lectures in some of the other famous colleges - St. John, Christ, Selwyn, Clare and Trinity Colleges - I recall. We also did an enormous amount of physical exercise, training and marching on the 'Backs' by the River Cam - always attracting dozens, if not scores, of onlookers, including many young ladies! The tests for Morse Code, Navigation, Aldis Lamp and Engineering were quite stiff and a small number from each squad would fail and were posted away as possible Air Gunners or Bomb Aimers. I enjoyed the stay at Cambridge and felt really fit and ready for the flying training part to follow.

FLYING TRAINING

No.17 EFTS, RAF Peterborough

On 9th July 1941, a small number of us were posted to RAF Peterborough and No.17 EFTS (Elementary Flying Training School) and so started our first insight into flying - in the world-famous DH82A, better known as the De Havilland Tiger Moth. The School had only moved to Peterborough that month from its original base at North Luffenham and as a Class A+1 School it catered for 150 pupil pilots and had 90 Tiger Moth IIs on strength.

My first-ever experience of flying was as a passenger in Tiger Moth T5698 on 19th July 1941; Sergeant Reed was my instructor and the first flight was called Air Experience and Familiarity with cockpit layout, and lasted just 20 minutes. I had another 30-minute flight in the same aircraft, the same day, with the same instructor – 'Effect of Controls and Taxying'. All very exciting stuff I seem to remember. Next day was in a different aircraft (T7026) but the same instructor and another 30-minute flight, this time 'Effect of Controls and Straight and Low Level Flight'. On 21st July I flew with Sgt. McDonald on 'Climbing, Side Slipping and Stall', which lasted 40 minutes. I was with Sgt. McDonald again the next day for another 40 minutes on 'Medium Turns and Taking-off into Wind'. This type of instruction continued for another 11 or 12 flights, mostly with Sgt. McDonald, although I flew with a Sgt. Spiers on 2nd August. The latter was for me a big, big day, for after 9 hours of instruction I was given a 25-minute test by Pilot Officer Roxburgh, who passed me for my first solo flight. It lasted just 10 minutes in Tiger Moth T5840 - oh, what joy that I could at last fly on my own. I landed without incident and was passed OK. It was a great feeling to go solo but a bit like treading water as you came in to land, half a hiccup and you bounce all over the place! I made two more flights that day, with one solo of 15 minutes, and one with Sgt Spiers with 35 minutes of low flying.

Wonderful day, the 2nd of August 1941 - I flew 5 times; two of which were solo. This carried on until 20th August, flying solo or instruction, mostly now with Sgt Spiers.

On 20th August Flying Officer Debenham took me up for a Flight Commander Test for one hour. I passed out with 'Average' assessment having carried-out 50 hours 5 minutes flying in the Tiger Moth. It had certainly been very hard work, with really no time off. There were two incidents that stick out in my memory - apart, of course, from the actual first solo, which for every pilot has a really special feeling. One incident, I recall, was going on a long-distance flight with Sgt Spiers. Peterborough Airfield was almost alongside the main East Coast railway line from London to Scotland, and one long straight stretch of track was where, in pre-war days, steam trains could reach over 100 miles per hour. We were flying into the wind and unofficially flying very low alongside the rail track, side by side with a very fast-travelling passenger train, and having difficulty keeping pace with it. Many of the passengers were waving, and as we got lower and lower and almost along side the locomotive, the fireman was standing in the coal tender and (jokingly) throwing large pieces of coal at us, missing of course: all in good fun and very exciting!

The other incident, again with the same instructor, came on another longish flight. Unbeknown to me he was taking some papers to be delivered to the De Havilland Airfield at Hatfield. We landed and he delivered the papers. On the other side of the airfield he pointed out to me a (then) very secret aircraft. He said it was a fast new bomber - very light and made of wood. We weren't allowed near, but we certainly saw it, and didn't know until a couple of years or so later that it was one of the early prototypes of the famous De Havilland Mosquito.

There were a small number of pupils, who for one reason or another failed the course, and some never made the going solo part. Off they went, never to be heard of by us again. There was always an element of nerves on a course, but as a youngster you cope and get on with it.

No.8 SFTS, RAF Montrose

We left Peterborough on 30th August 1941 for a one-week leave to await posting to a Service Flying Training School (SFTS). This was before the vast Empire Air Training Scheme came into being so we were pretty certain to be posted somewhere in the United Kingdom. Those of us who had passed and had been selected to train as Fighter Pilots (on single engined aircraft) were either sent to No.8 SFTS or one of the other Service Flying Training Schools allocated to this task.

On the 11th of September 1941, I was posted to Montrose on the East Coast of Scotland. There were some 25 to 30 U/T (Under Training) pilots on my course, including a dozen or so Army Officers of varying rank, who had volunteered to convert to the RAF if they were successful on the Course. Also there were a small number of qualified Polish Air Force Pilots of varying rank, who really kept themselves to themselves. They always seemed to be jabbering loudly whether in the air or on the ground. However, after we got to know them better, we found out that they were very experienced pilots (in the pre-war Polish Air Force) - but they had to go through our thorough training and learn our ways, which they did.

After a very long dreary train journey from London, several of us arrived at Montrose station, and were collected by an RAF truck and taken through the small town of Montrose. As we were about to enter the gates of RAF Montrose (a long-standing Training Airfield established before World War One), we had to give way to a funeral procession going to the nearby church and graveyard. It appeared that earlier in the week, during night flying, a pupil-pilot in a Miles Master had collided with an Avro Anson trainer aircraft, which was about to land. All five people were killed. Not a very pleasant start to our time at Montrose! Flying training has always had its share of accidents, many of them fatal, and it was very unusual for a course not to have at least one fatality. In a perverse way this helped us come to terms with losing colleagues – something that would be all too frequent on an operational squadron.

Still, we were so busy with striving to master what we were being taught, and to pass the Course, that there was no time to dwell on such incidents.

For me, flying started on 15th September in a Miles Master Mark I with Sgt Griffiths as my instructor. After nine flights in just six days I was tested and went solo (21st September). There followed a further 80 or so flying hours, including approximately 43 solo flights, in Miles Master I and II aircraft under various instructors before completing the Course on 26th February 1942. Night flying was the worse time and was the cause of many accidents – and deaths. I recall on one night solo trip I overshot to make another circuit, entered cloud and became disoriented. This was a very dangerous situation and was often put down as the cause of fatal crashes. I don't remember how much I panicked or how I got out of it, but somehow I cheated fate and ended up back on the runway in one piece! The Master II was an excellent training aircraft and after the Tiger Moth it seemed to us to be like a fighter, and had the same exhilaration when you flew it solo – which of course was the whole point. It seemed a massive aircraft and far more solid after the Tiger and very fast. We always made 3-point landings and you had to settle it in, which was good training for a Spitfire as the technique was the same; by the end of my Spitfire period I could drop the aircraft down on a spot. There were a few Hurricanes at the School and in the latter stages of the Course some chaps got to fly these, which, as we all thought we were heading for fighters, would have been a nice end to the Course.

During the Course we suffered some very severe weather hold-ups, including days of fog and mists when flying was impossible; also several snow storms that stopped us from flying for many days. On one occasion a number of local villages were cut off by snow, and we were dispatched to help dig a way through - some drifts were well over 12 feet high.

After a while we were taken by truck each morning to a nearby satellite airfield called Stracathro - just a field, no runways - to practise take-offs and landings. The Course seemed to go on forever because of the bad weather delays. Night flying was an extremely nervous time for us all, with fog and Scotch mist, which would suddenly form, blanketing out the airfield, and we were always wary of being caught up in them. We, and two or three other courses all had a small number of fatalities and I think all of us who passed the Course successfully, considered ourselves lucky. We were indeed pleased to get our wings - and our Sergeants stripes. No commissions were awarded because the allocation was already taken up by the ex-Army Officers and Poles! No Wings Parade or anything. We were simply instructed to go to the stores and collect our wings and stripes. We were further told to make sure that we personally sew them onto our tunic the right way up. I think we were all able to find a friendly WAAF who did the necessary sewing for us. Whatever happened to the splendid Wings Day Parades you saw on the films? Each pilot's name would be called out and they marched up to the platform where some Top Brass pinned their wings onto their tunic in front of all the families and loved ones. No such luck for us!

Whilst we were at Montrose, 603 Squadron (which was based at nearby Dyce, Aberdeen) had a flight of Spitfires based at Montrose, a small number of aircraft always at readiness. It was very exciting when they were scrambled to intercept unidentified aircraft. The Squadron was commanded by a well known personality of the day - a Squadron Leader, the Duke of Hamilton - who was married to Prunella Stack, head of the `Woman's League of Health and Beauty'. It was said that whenever she was at the airfield, she would have all the 603 Squadron pilots strip off to their shorts in the bitterly cold weather and make them perform physical jerks (with a view to keeping them fit I suppose). I must admit that I never saw any of these performing pilots, as it could have been quite a sight!

One or two memories of Montrose come to mind. A Sergeant Pilot who had been my instructor on the early morning flight was about to take me up again for navigation instruction when he was suddenly told to take another pilot instead. They crashed into nearby mountains in bad weather and were both killed. I also recall that on nonflying days (usually due to bad weather) some of us would walk into Montrose and enjoy a cup of tea and nice cakes at Mary's Tea Shop - Scotland didn't seem to have many pubs, or at least not as we knew them in England.

We left Montrose on 28th February 1942, fully qualified pilots but with few flying hours. The Officer Commanding Flying Wing at Montrose endorsed our flying books with a certificate. Mine read:

> *Proficiency as Pilot on Type* – Average
> *Has he shown aptitude as a Pilot/Navigator* – Yes
> *Night Visual Acuity* – Above Average
> *Signed: S/L J F McKenna AFC*

Most of us were pleased to get away from cold and foggy Montrose all in one piece. The next move was to one of the Fighter OTUs (Operational Training Units). We were sent home for a couple of weeks leave to await the telegram indicating where and when to report. I must say I was feeling rather proud in my Sergeants stripes and new pilot's wings.

No.55 OTU (Operational Training Unit), RAF Usworth

I was instructed to report to No.55 OTU at a place called Usworth near Washington on the 17th March 1942. At first I thought it was Washington in the USA - because the new aircrew training schemes were coming into effect and many were being sent to Canada and the USA, also Rhodesia and South Africa. However, closer inspection showed it was Washington near Newcastle!

Flying started on the 24th March, with a sector reconnaissance in a Tiger Moth piloted by a Flt Lt Askew. The next day was dual instruction in a Miles Master Mark I by Flt Lt Rippon with so called "dual landings" for just 25 minutes. Then it was off to the Hurricane and total awe of the aircraft when first seen close up; the first thing being to sit in the cockpit and get used to the controls and layout. There was no dual-control Hurricane, so you were on your own from the first flight. This was followed immediately by my first flight in Hawker Hurricane Mark I (6622) for circuits and landings lasting one hour 10 minutes; later the same day I was up again in the same Hurricane Mk I for 'experience on type and sector recce', a trip that lasted one hour 35 minutes. Quite a day! Once you opened the throttle it pushed you into the seat as you roared off down the runway. As always, landing was the trickiest part and we tended to land rolling on main wheels, so it was important to keep the nose up and the brakes off, or an embarrassing tip-up on the nose would result (and maybe worse). It was also important to remember to put the undercarriage down, so you always kept a look-out for a red Verey from the ground that would wave you off, usually because the gear was not down! Formation flying was tricky until you were experienced, and on early flights you tended to pump the throttle and see-saw until you settled down.

No flying on 26th March, but three flights the next day:

Handling practise and landings - 1 hour 5 minutes.
DF Homings and Cross Country -1 hour 40 minutes.
Cross country - 1 hour 15 minutes.

A splendid total of 4 hours in one day! This pattern was followed most days as there was pressure to graduate pilots as quickly as possible. One day, the 22nd April, I was sent up seven times for mostly air-to-air and air-to-ground firing; again a total of almost 4 hours.

Looking back after all these years, it's now pretty hard to remember much of the nature of the very short periods devoted to air-to-air and air-to-ground firing. The Hurricane I armament consisted of eight 0.303-in machine guns – four mounted in each wing and it was only on a couple of occasions that live ammo was used against ground targets; I can only assume that we shot at drogues for air-to-air. Ground firing (I think) was low level approach (not diving) onto the target on firing ranges, and, of course air-to-air required allowing for deflection. Most of the other firing – air-to-air – was cine camera. Again, if I remember correctly, most of us were concerned that not enough time was devoted to the subject of firing and gunnery on the Course, which for potential fighter pilots seemed short-sighted.

I suspect that part of reason for all the hassle and speed to complete the Course was because on 22nd April (the day of seven flights) we were told to pack our kit and be ready to fly over to RAF Annan, which was near Carlisle on the Scottish Borders. On 29th April we actually moved to Annan and the rush started again. The OTU had officially moved to Annan on the 28th and used the satellite airfield at Longtown to ease the training workload. At this time it had an establishment of 75 Hurricanes, 22 Masters, and a small number of target-towing types. One of the main problems we had was serviceability, as the Hurricanes were generally worn-out ex operational aircraft, and I pitied the poor old groundcrew who had to keep them going.

In early May it was back on the Master for a while for Instrument Flying (IF) in cloud and more low flying. This was followed by final Hurricane trips and the end of the course on 10th May, by which time I had flown 53 hours 30 minutes in Hurricane Is, plus a few more in Masters. We were now ready to join a front line Squadron.

The rather rushed course at Usworth and Annan was occasionally interspersed by the odd day off. It was interesting to note that whenever any of us ventured into the pubs in the small village of Usworth we were almost snubbed by the locals, who were mostly connected with the coal-mining industry. They seemed to live in a dream world and gave the impression that the war was nothing to do with them. In fact, they (the miners) came out on strike for more pay whilst we were there. The Commanding Officer of Usworth offered to show any of the miners who wished, around the airfield and take a short flight in one of the Miles Masters. I believe some did and they in turn offered to take us down one of the mines. Some of us, I believe, did go. Eventually I think there was a better understanding between us.

At Annan there wasn't much time to get away for the day, except to go into Carlisle for a few beers, although we did visit Gretna Green once. A number of the instructors were ex Battle of Britain pilots, including some well-known aces, the idea being that they could talk to us and pass on general knowledge about life on an operational squadron. This was all right for the few commissioned pupil pilots, but for the majority of us NCO pilots, who lived in a different Mess, it was not so convenient. I have always considered the segregation of Commissioned and NCO pilots was a huge mistake, especially on an operational squadron. The Americans, of course, had the right idea - all pilots were commissioned, although much later in the war they seemed to introduce non-commissioned pilots in certain non-operational capacities. However, at the dispersal or flight areas we did, of course, meet up. The instructors were all super guys!

The Wing Commander Flying at No.55 OTU during my stay was Wg Cdr W. D. David DFC and Bar, who survived the war to end as a Group Captain; sadly passing away at the age of 83 in September 2000. One of the instructors was Flt Lt J. J. Le Roux DFC and two Bars, who was the Flight Commander of the flight I was in - `D' Flight. He was a South African and was killed on operations in North Africa in September 1944 - his final score being 23 destroyed. Another, Flying Officer Francis Eckford DFC, also an instructor in `D' Flight, survived the war, his final score being eight destroyed. He did three operational tours, eventually becoming the CO of 242 Squadron in Italy. All of the instructors, including NCOs, had survived at least one tour of operations in fighter squadrons.

It had been an extremely busy and hard-working flying Course, but we were all raring to go and wondering to which fighter Squadron we would have to report and indeed what theatre of war - Middle East, Far East or a Home posting. We left Annan for a week's leave again to await the vital telegram to say where we were to end up.

FIRST TOUR – No. 80 SQUADRON

It was almost two years from the day I entered RAF service at Cardington in (June 1940) when in May 1942 I was posted to RAF Wilmslow PTC (Personnel Transit Centre). We were all kitted out with tropical gear and those old fashioned pith helmets, so we all knew it was to be the Middle or Far East. But, oh no! They were not to tell us where - we'll find out when aboard ship!

On 30th May 1942 we boarded the train, which took us to Greenock on the River Clyde in Scotland. There were two batches, with approximately 50 of us in each batch. The first squad went out in a small boat and made directly for the USS *Wasp*, an American Aircraft Carrier. We heard later that they were to proceed into the Mediterranean and stop some 500 miles short of Malta (which was under siege at the time), and were to fly off the carriers in Spitfires (some pilots had only flown Hurricanes as I remember), to be led in several groups to Malta. Most arrived safely, but some ditched and were lost. Many of these pilots didn't survive the fierce air battles that raged for many months over the Island, until Malta was made safe by advancing armies following the drive from El Alamein, and also from the Algerian landings. We, of course, knew nothing of all this until much later in the war.

Our batch of roughly 50 pilots was sent out in a small boat and we went alongside and boarded the enormous battleship HMS *Nelson*, where we were made most welcome by the ship's very large crew. We were allocated two of the Chief Petty Officers' Messes to sleep, and eat, and we were to remain there unless taken on organised visits to the other parts of this huge vessel. The ship was very overcrowded because it was also carrying a complete cruiser crew to Freetown.

It was certainly a very interesting experience. The first week the weather in the Bay of Biscay was terrible. We did get up on deck once or twice and saw the huge convoy of ships, which included several aircraft carriers, including HMS *Argus*, which was especially notable as it was flying off some aircraft as we watched.

It took the convoy 2 or 3 weeks to reach Freetown in West Africa, as we apparently had to make a huge detour into the South Atlantic because of the U-Boat packs hunting the oceans. Eventually we tied up alongside *Nelson's* sister battleship, HMS *Rodney*, and the language and shouts and behaviour from the two great ships' crews was something to be believed. The *Nelson* was a most interesting ship to be on, and we were eventually allowed to wander over the ship at will when we entered the tropics and better weather, although they preferred us to move about in small groups. We (the small RAF contingent) became most popular with the Navy boys, mainly, I believe, because some of our chaps entered for sports events being organised by the sailors - the most memorable being a boxing tournament between the Navy and RAF. My friends and I kept out of the way, of course, having absolutely no knowledge of the art of boxing! As luck would have it, our party included one guy who turned out to be the RAF Boxing Champion of his area. There were also others who were good boxers and the RAF team beat the Navy hands down. We all (RAF) seemed to be very popular after that!

We disembarked at Freetown and left our new-found Navy friends, transferring to a small coaster to go a few hundred miles down the coast to a place called Takoradi, arriving there on 24th June 1942.

Takoradi was a RAF Transit Airfield for ferrying aircraft and people across Africa to the Middle East Theatre. There we had extra jabs as malaria was rampant in the area. On the 4th July we left Takoradi in a Pan American Airway's Dakota DC-2 (converted for troop carrying) en route for Cairo. This took five days, arriving in Cairo on 9th July. The journey was a very tedious, swelteringly hot affair, requiring stops for fuel and overnight rest as follows:

4ᵗʰ July Boarded DC-2, Pilot Captain Murray.

4ᵗʰ July Takoradi to Kano, 5 hours 20 minutes.

4ᵗʰ July Kano to Maidugare one hour 50 minutes.

5ᵗʰ July Maidugare to El Fasher 4 hours 55 minutes.

5ᵗʰ July El Fasher to Wadi Seidna (Khartoum) 3 hours.

9ᵗʰ July Wadi Seidna to Heliopolis 6 hours 35 minutes.

I seem to recall that our delay on the 6th, 7th and 8th was caused by problems with the DC-2, and that we were free each day to have a look at Khartoum, which was a horrible place – too bloody hot - and we were glad to be moving on! I am not sure of the spelling of some of these airfields but they are as I recorded them at the time in my log book.

We spent the next two months at a terrible place called Almaza on the outskirts of Cairo, with No.22 PTC (Personnel Transit Camp). We were all billeted in small tents in desert conditions, doing absolutely nothing - just waiting for that all-important posting. Almaza was a small town and was served by a quite-frequent train/tramway service - two or three trams attached together as a train, and we used it as often as we could to get away from No.22 PTC. These trams were most extraordinary as they were always grossly overcrowded. The locals filled the cars to overflowing with many of them sitting on the roof and hundreds, literally, clinging onto the sides. Hardly a journey went by without someone being knocked off or falling off the tram as they sped along, especially as two trams passed each other. It was always a horrific journey. Personally I hated Cairo, especially the amount of squalor to be found there. The best bars and hotels were off limits to NCOs (all other ranks actually), as they were always reserved for officers. The whole place was teaming with troops and it seemed as if the whole of the 8th Army was there, including the many thousands of Australian and New Zealand troops. It was at the time when Rommel was successfully pushing us back to the El Alamein area; low morale and a general air of despondency was about.

We did find some interesting places to visit, especially by the River Nile. Quite a number of boating and sports clubs were open to even us miserable NCO people, so it really wasn't all bad. I remember that at Almaza we were required to attend a parade each morning. This took place at 10 o'clock and was to ascertain whether we had a posting; if not, then the rest of the day was free, – the only requirement being that we return to camp by 2359 hours. For me, Cairo and this spell of waiting was the worst period so far in the RAF.

Marvellous news! On the 7th of September 1942, several of my colleagues and I were posted to a place called El Ballah, a RAF airfield right by the side of the Suez Canal and home to No.1 METS (Middle East Training School). This was for a short refresher course – 7 days of lectures, followed by 5 days of flying with 12 flights in Hurricane Is, totalling 9 hours 5 minutes. This consisted of circuits and landings, area recce, air-to-ground firing, cine-camera attacks and formation flying. I suppose this was quite useful in view of the fact that I had last flown an aircraft at OTU on 10th May 1942!

I remember that the CO of 'B' Flight Advanced Flying School at El Ballah was a Canadian Flt Lt named Conrad; later to become Wg Cdr W.A.G. Conrad DFC and Bar, serving in the European Theatre. He was to survive the war after three operational tours. Also at El Ballah was another Canadian, a Flight Lieutenant named Keefer, who also became a Wg Cdr, and ended up with a DSO and Bar, DFC and Bar: he and 'Wally'Conrad were great friends.

Unfortunately, back we came to Almaza for another month, 19th September to 17th October 1942. More waiting and hanging about. Then, surprisingly, a few of us were sent on a 10-day leave period on a Nile houseboat known as ADV HQ. I don't remember too much about this period, but I do remember it was a welcome change to being stuck in sand and tents. The houseboat, which was quite large, was based on the banks of the Nile and used as a leave venue for RAF Aircrews - very welcome!

The abbreviation ADV HQ usually stands for Advanced Headquarters and may have been used in this context as something of an RAF joke, suggesting that the 'powers that be' stayed in relative luxury away from the front-line!

We were back again to No.22 PTC Almaza on the 27th of October, but this time only for a few days, and then a more interesting move to the Western Desert at Wadi Natrun and No.25 PTC for 3 days, from the 1st to the 4th November 1942. We were getting closer to the front-line, but still with no sign of a posting to a squadron. The next move was to LG 203 (Landing Ground 203) and No.1 RSU (Repair and Salvage Unit). No.1 RSU was a Repair and Salvage Unit for No.7 South African Air Force Wing, and we were to be based with the unit until required to replace a pilot on a squadron. While waiting, and to keep us from getting bored, we also test flew the various Hurricane aircraft following repairs caused by battle or accident damage.

This was the period of the El Alamein offensive, which commenced at 8 p.m. on the 23rd of October and led to a final breakthrough on 4th November. The enemy resistance crumbled and the battered Germans and their Italian allies began a 1,500-mile retreat. However, the British and Commonwealth forces lost 13,500 men and 500 tanks in just less than two weeks. El Alamein cemetery has 7,239 white crosses to mark the graves of those whose bodies were recovered; a memorial to many brave men who sacrificed their lives for this victory.

We seemed to be moving about every few days:

4th -16th November - LG 203

16th -23rd November – LG012 Sidi Haneish North

23-26th November - Tmimi

26th November to 9th January 1943 - Gazala No. 3

Most of the time we spent testing and delivering aircraft and collecting aircraft from various squadrons - approximately 10 hours flying in all. Three of us were granted 3 days leave in Cairo, which included a Christmas Day luncheon in a quite acceptable hotel. I recall the restaurant was a couple of floors up from the street and had quite a large dining area in a number of open-plan rooms. Our Christmas meal was very good and the waiters got rather carried away when it came to serving the Christmas Pudding. Our waiter doused the pudding with almost a bottle of brandy, which was far too much, and when he applied his lighter it burst into very large flames, which actually reached the ceiling. Despite our best efforts we were unable to blow out the flames, and they had to be put out by a fire extinguisher. So, we missed out on the pudding, which, by this time, was just a blackened soggy mess!

The rest of the meal was a great success. Just as we were about to leave the restaurant, however, the Christmas occasion was rather spoilt by an extremely rowdy party of Australian Army people who were having their meal in one of the other rooms. This room had access to a balcony, which overlooked the main street. Their dinner party was getting out of hand - too much drink, I suppose - and just as we were leaving, the Aussies started to move an upright piano out onto the balcony. The piano was pushed out over the balcony and it crashed down into the street and broke up. Thankfully no one was hurt, but we beat a hasty retreat because the Military Police were already descending on the scene. We didn't want to get mixed up in that mess! However, all in all, it was quite a good couple of days off for Christmas in Cairo.

We returned to an airfield called El Adam on 26th December in a Lodestar aircraft as passengers, and returned to our own airfield by truck. I had one last flight in a Hurricane (6th January 1943) before I was at long last posted to a squadron; my destination as a replacement pilot was to 80 Squadron RAF, then part of No. 7 SAAF Wing at Sidi Bu Amud, near Tobruk.

Operational with 80 Squadron

I thought back to the day that I volunteered for pilot training in the RAF, the 7th of

March 1940 (my 18th birthday) and now, at long, long last I was joining 80 Squadron as an inexperienced Sergeant Pilot on 9th January 1943 – taking nearly 2 ¾ years to get this far!.

Although I didn't appreciate it at the time, 80 Squadron was one of the top fighter squadrons in the Western Desert, first flying Gloster Gladiators and now Hawker Hurricanes. What I also didn't know at the time was the fact that after going through very heavy fighting, in the ebb and flow of the long Desert War, and during the infamous Greek Campaign, it had produced a number of exceptional pilots. The most famous of these was Flt Lt `Pat' Pattle, who served with 80 Squadron in North Africa and Greece until he was promoted to Squadron Leader to command 33 Squadron on 23rd March 1941, the other fighter unit in the Greek campaign. He was shot-down and killed on 20th April 1941, his aircraft falling into Piraeus Bay, Athens. His final credited score was over 40 victories, but may have been much higher. Indeed, some of the personnel who survived the Greek Campaign consider it to be nearer 60 destroyed, but there is no real doubt that he was the highest-scoring fighter pilot in the RAF and Commonwealth Air Forces, and 80 Squadron was rightly proud of him.

Another famous 80 Squadron pilot was Flt Lt 'Imshi' Mason, who was later killed flying with 94 Squadron, his total score being 17 victories. Several pilots achieved Air Rank in later years after serving for a time with 80 Squadron. John Hugh Lapsley was the CO at one stage and died in 1995 after achieving the rank of Air Marshal (total score of 11 victories). Air Marshal Sir Peter Wickham, who also died in 1995, was an early flyer with 80 Squadron, and several NCO pilots achieved `stardom'. For example, Hewitt, who by the end of the war was a Squadron Leader Commanding 263 Squadron flying Typhoons, achieved a final score of 21 victories. So I was definitely joining one of the best fighter outfits!

After returning from Greece, 80 Squadron moved up and down, or rather back and forth, over the Western Desert, supporting Eighth Army, and on 9th January 1943 they were, it appears, re-forming at an airstrip in the desert at a location called Bu Amud - not far from Tobruk. This proved to be a quiet spell for the Squadron and it became part of the force guarding the very long supply line from Malta to Alexandria and Cairo, and was engaged in convoy patrols with the occasional recce or air strike on targets in the Western Desert or even Crete and Rhodes. It was also involved in trying to intercept the high flying Ju 88s that came over almost daily to spy on, and photograph, our shipping movements.

When I look back at this 'quiet period' I realise I was very lucky to be able to gain experience and fit into the way of Squadron life in the less active flying period, as opposed to dog-fighting or being troubled with massive flak when attacking ground targets. I believe this probably helped me to survive those early days on an operational Squadron. I remained with 80 Squadron from 9th January 1943 to 23rd August 1944, and whilst the first period was quiet, there was plenty of action to come.

So it was, on that early January day, I was introduced to all the pilots, including an interview with the then CO, Sqn Ldr D.M. Jack, who at the end of the month handed over to a new CO, Sqn Ldr R.E. Bary DFC. He remained our CO until July 1943 when a rather different type of CO arrived - Sqn Ldr J.H. 'Crash' Curry DFC. He was a most unusual character and was shot-down by flak when we were operating in Italy (2nd March 1944 and became a PoW) – but more about 'Crash' Curry later.

On 11th January 1943 I made my first flight in an 80 Squadron Hurricane IIc – a trip of one hour 5 minutes, surveying the area around the airfield to get the 'lay of the land' so to speak. The next trip was three days later - this time something called `shadow firing'. I am not too sure what `shadow firing' actually was but it probably involved firing at my aircraft's shadow reflected in the desert sand!

My next five flights were operation on convoy patrols:

> *18th January* -2 hours 10 minutes.
> *19th January* - 2 hours 15 minutes.
> *22nd January* - 1 hour 35 minutes.
> *22nd January* - 1 hour 45 minutes.
> *24th January* - 2 hours 20 minutes.

Nothing much can have happened on these flights as there is nothing of note in my log book.

Another convoy patrol on 30th January for one hour 30 minutes and then later the same day I was on `standby' - strapped in and sweating in the cockpit. I was scrambled to intercept an unidentified aircraft and landed after 45 minutes. With no comment in my log book it was obviously a friendly aircraft or I didn't find anything. I flew on another convoy patrol later in the day. The following day I had two flights, both on formation practise. This type of sortie was a regular part of our routine as it was important that we kept up our formation skills.

February started with more convoy patrols and I flew nine in all during the month, interspersed with practise flying of all sorts, including one scramble to check an unidentified aircraft, with no recorded conclusion. Night flying took place from 17th to 19th and included a cross country route: base - Sollum - Raz Azziz - El Aden -base. It was always 'interesting' navigating at night over the desert! February ended with more convoy patrols and practise flying, and this pattern was kept up throughout March including, on 12th March, convoy patrols, one scramble and much practise flying. Thankfully, we flew our last convoy patrol on 2nd April, a day that saw another uneventful scramble and a squadron sweep over the sea.

Many of our convoy patrols consisted of dawn to dusk cover by two of our aircraft over one or other of the two Navy Minesweepers - HMS *Manxman* or HMS *Welshman*. These were very fast ships and made a solo dash from Alexandria to Malta and back. Malta was under siege at the time and hardly any ships or convoys were getting through. I recall on one occasion Sgt Tom Chambers and I were on dawn (first) patrol over the *Manxman* - we usually flew around 10,000 feet above the ship. On this particular day, we were just about to be relieved by the next two Hurricanes, when my colleague foolishly decided to dive down on the rear of the *Manxman* and pull up over the ship and away - in a sort of friendly gesture - for we had been patrolling overhead for some 2 hours or so. I just stood by and watched as Tom pulled up from his `friendly' dive and began to climb away over the ship. There was a puff of smoke from one of the ship's guns and Tom was hit and his plane set on fire, at about 1,000 feet or so. Tom turned his plane over and baled-out and landed in the sea. The *Manxman*, which was travelling at 30-35 knots just wheeled round in a large circle and steered at the same speed right by Tom in the water, and literally fished him up on board without stopping and took him on to Malta. I sat above rapidly trying to think of what to say when I returned alone ... some sort of tale of an engine problem seemed best. Actually, I do not now recall what I said – but I don't remember any trouble from it. Anyway, a week or so later Tom returned, saying what a marvellous time he had on board - plenty of rum and dry clothes - and he was returned to us none the worse for wear. For the life of me I can't remember whether he was summoned to appear in front of a Courts Martial or what, but he remained with the Squadron for quite a long time afterwards.

Some 15 years ago I related this story to a neighbour of mine, a retired Commander in the Navy. After I'd finished the tale, he said he was an officer on HMS *Manxman* in the Mediterranean at this time and remembered `some idiot' who dived down on the rear of his ship "so we naturally shot him down" - quite a coincidence!

I well remember 7th March 1943 - my 21st birthday. I managed to celebrate by drinking, during the day, two bottles of Seagram V.O. Canadian Whisky. The bottles had a small yellowish band of material around the neck of the bottle. After I'd finished off the two bottles, my colleagues used this to make an insignia of a medal resembling the DFC or DFM. They presented me with what they called the VO and Bar for meritorious drinking on my 21st birthday! I am afraid I was flat out (totally legless) and was finally carried off to my tent to sleep it off - luckily I didn't have to fly again until 9th March! I'm not sure of the date, but around this time our beloved Pilots' Mess was unfortunately burnt down. All the chairs, tables and most of the drink were lost - could this have been the time of my 21st birthday? I have photographs of the fire and also photographs of myself, and others, inside the Mess during my birthday celebrations, all looking rather the worse for wear!

It was during March that my Flight Commander, an Australian by the name of Fosket, left us to become the CO of 94 Squadron. A quote from the book 'Ace's High' records:

"FOSKET, RUSSELL GEORGE, was an Australian from Sydney. He joined the RAAF in September 1940 and joined No.80 Squadron in the Western Desert in June 1941, flying Hurricanes as a Sergeant. On 24th November he shot down a Bf 110 and got another of these on 16th January 1942. He was commissioned in March and on 20th April shared in the destruction of a Bf 109. He destroyed another Bf 109 on 10th July, during the month became a Flight Commander. During November he shot-down two Ju 87s in one sortie and the following month received the DFC. In March 1943, he left 80 Squadron and was rested from operations and in October was posted to 94 Squadron in the Eastern Mediterranean, again flying Hurricanes. In March 1944 he became Commanding Officer and in June converted to Spitfire IXs. On 6th June he shot down a Ju 52 bringing his score to 6½ with 2 probables and 4 damaged. He damaged a Bf 109 on 10th August but on 31st October had engine failure over the Greek Islands. He baled out, but was not found and was reported missing, presumed killed." I remember Russ, he treated us NCO pilots very well and encouraged us in every way - we all thought the world of him - a truly fine Australian.

The 15th of April 1943 was a great day for the Squadron for we said `good-bye' to our faithful Hurricane IIC's, and we were overjoyed to have delivered to us Spitfire VCs - not necessarily brand new, but none the less welcome. We also had a Harvard aircraft, and Sqn Ldr Bary decided to take each pilot up and test us on circuits and landings, prior to us flying the Spitfire for the first time. So on 15th April I suffered one hour 10 minutes of circuits and landings with the CO in the Harvard. Everything must have gone OK, because the next day was my first flight in a Spitfire VC: one hour 25 minutes of local flying. What sheer joy!!

The Spitfire was much more manoeuvrable than the Hurricane and could out-climb it and get higher, and with its reputation it was one of those aircraft that all fighter pilots wanted to fly. However, the Hurricane was a much sturdier beast, and we reckoned that in a forced-landing it would go through a house, whereas the Spitfire would simply crumple!

The rest of April was filled with flying the Spitfire around the area, doing all sorts of formation practise, air-to-air, air-to-ground and, yes, the odd spell of readiness, including one scramble, which again amounted to nothing found. On 22nd April some of us flew from Bu Amud to Gambut 3 and did fighter affiliation for the Baltimore aircraft stationed there - practise for them rather than us. It was a full day, and we were late returning back at base that night.

We continued practise flying, including Squadron formation, plus one scramble, this time to 28,000 feet - quite high for those days - but as soon as the wretched photographic Ju.188 saw us, it put its nose down and belted for the sea and returned to Greece, where presumably it was based.

Life in the desert, apart from the flying, was very mundane. There was really no place to go when off-duty except the Mess, which was a large marquee where all the pilots, including NCO pilots and all officers at the base ate and relaxed. On a number of occasions we suffered heavy sand-storms, with gale force winds, when we had to stay put in our own, very small ridge-type tents or somehow find our way over to the main Pilots' Mess. These sand-storms usually lasted for a day or two and we were completely demoralised by them. Sand got into everything - eyes, nose, mouth - sand everywhere, and it was most unpleasant. We also suffered heavy rain at times, which waterlogged the airfield, sometimes washing into the small living space in our ridge tents. Other times we were able, if off-duty, to get a truck to the beach and enjoy a swim or two, but this was not possible very often. Every so often an RAF dentist would turn up at the camp with a van and trailer and we had to line-up to see him. His main piece of equipment, the drill, was powered by an Arab assistant who pedalled away madly to power the contraption. It was a somewhat unusual 'power drill' – but not one as we know it today! Having a surname with a 'J', I was not near the front of the queue and by the time my turn came the poor old pedaller was somewhat worn-out. The conclusion was that I needed four fillings, but in the absence of a drill that became four extractions!

May 1943 still found us at Bu Amud, mainly practise flying with the odd scramble thrown in, never amounting to much. Then on 15th May we left Bu Amud having spent just over four months there, a long time in terms of Western Desert operations.

We flew via Mersa Matruh to Idku, which was to be our new home for almost two months. Idku was away from the Western Desert, between Alexandria and Suez. It was at this stage that Sqn Ldr Bary left us, and we were presented with an entirely different `type' of CO, Sqn Ldr John Harvey Curry DFC.

An extract from 'Ace's High' records: "He was from Dallas, Texas. He was a barnstorming pilot before the war and in 1940 joined the RCAF. He was later posted to the United Kingdom, joining 601 Squadron. Known as 'Crash', he was a Flight Commander by April 1942 when the Squadron was posted to Malta. He fought on the island until July and the Squadron was moved to the Western Desert. Here on

1st September he shot-down two Bf 109s and on the 7th claimed another damaged. On 9th he probably destroyed a Bf 109 and damaged a Macchi 202. He probably destroyed another Bf 109 on 11th October and on 21st shot-down a Macchi 202. He destroyed another of these on 26th - his seventh victory. He received the DFC in March 1943, and after a rest from operations, commanded 80 Squadron. His total score at the end of the war was 8."

We had a great deal of respect for 'Crash' Curry. He set about really putting us through our paces with 'tail-chasing'. A small formation of say four aircraft went off and he would do all sorts of attacks on us, 'out of the sun', 'up and under' and really gave us a hard time. He was a magnificent pilot, nobody could touch him - remember he had his own 'Flying Circus' in Texas before the war. He did not approve of the RAF gun sight and had his own built into his aircraft. He was out 'polishing' his Spitfire almost every day until it gleamed, and no airman was allowed to go near it. He was always immaculately dressed, even in desert conditions and, as I have said, was very well respected by his pilots - and that's where it ended. As far as NCO Pilots were concerned, he appeared to have no time whatsoever for any of us, and I can't remember ever talking to him. As for recommending anyone for a commission, I don't think it ever occurred to him. He remained with us until 2nd March 1944 when he was shot-down on operations in Italy, and after a long time evading capture, was finally made a POW.

Our stay at Idku was, apart from this intensive flying training, taken-up by a continuous readiness by two of us each day in shifts, in two special Spitfires with reduced weight - no armour - just two cannons and specially-extended wing tips and four-blade props. All this to try to enable us to gain the maximum height to combat the daily appearance of the photo-reconnaissance Ju 188 aircraft that the Germans sent over to spy on the shipping in Alexandria, and other locations. On one such scramble on 20th March my Leader and I climbed to 31,000 feet, but we were unable to close on the Ju 188 because he was two or three thousand feet above, and as soon as he saw us would just dive away back to his base in Greece. I was on four other such scrambles, with again height being the problem. On one occasion we were able to make a head-on attack from just below the Ju 188, but as soon as our guns were fired our speed and height were lost and again he got away. Very frustrating! The best result we could hope for was to frighten him and curtail whatever reconnaissance he was on.

Just to mention something about Idku. The airfield was just west of Alexandria on the coast road to Rosetta, and I imagine it was an old Navy airfield; quite small with the main road running across part of the airfield. All traffic had to be held up whenever we were taking-off or landing, and it was not an easy airfield to land on because of its small size. In quite a poor district, run-down huts or dwellings surrounded the airfield, and a very high barbed-wire fence was extended entirely around the airfield and its buildings. I believe quite a number of local people either worked on the airfield or were allowed to enter through the gates each day.

We were billeted in small EPIP tents housing about 6 to 8 of us in each. In spite of the high wire fencing and gates there was an awful amount of stealing of anything the locals could lay their hands on. For instance, I remember on a number of occasions people woke up in the mornings to find their tents had been stolen whilst they were asleep! How they did this is still a mystery. To take down a largish tent and take it away over the wire fence was really amazing. This happened to our tent during one night, and we lost much of our gear as well.

We were able to make the odd trip into Alexandria, which I thought was more interesting than Cairo. I remember on one occasion while walking along one of Alexandria's streets by the sea I bumped into a cousin of mine who was serving in the Army and we were able to spend a few hours talking of old times. I also suffered a very horrible, but thankfully, short spell of the famous 'Gyppo stomach'. I was so bad that I was taken by ambulance to the Navy Hospital in Alexandria. It seemed to clear up after a couple of days and so I discharged myself and found my way back to the Squadron at Idku. Overall, Idku was a horrible place, and we were all pleased to get away from it.

On 5ᵗʰ July the Squadron moved in formation from Idku to Savoia by way of Mersa Matruh and El Adem, with a transit time of 3 hours 10 minutes. Savoia was back through the Western Desert to the cultivated area, developed by the Italians, near Cyrene in Apollonia. Our stay at Savoia lasted until 11ᵗʰ August 1943. Again it was back to convoy patrol plus the almost daily scramble for (usually) unidentified aircraft, and also more practice flying. Life at Savoia was still desert conditions but it was not too far from cultivated land. We still had our Pilots' Mess and, of course, slept in tents as before. We were able to move off base occasionally, by truck, either for swimming in the Mediterranean or for sight-seeing, a notable landmark being the large Roman amphitheatre at Cyrene, which was very interesting. On one occasion whilst travelling along the main coastal road we noticed that the sky appeared darkened. The whole area was literally blackened with a massive swarm of locusts that had descended on vast fields of crops and within a few minutes all flew off, completely devastating the crops of foliage. The mass flew right over us, and the road was thick with the squashed bodies of locusts run over by the heavy traffic. This was an amazing sight, and we experienced it once more before moving on again.

Our next move came as a complete surprise, for we assumed we would be following up in the general direction of where the war was at that time. Our forces were in Sicily and were preparing to go into the South of Italy. To our horror our next destination was a place called St Jean, which was perched high up near the top of Mount Carmel, and well beyond Haifa in Northern Palestine. It took us over 5 hours flying in three stages - Savoia to Mersa Matruh to Abu Sueir to St Jean. All this took place on 11ᵗʰ August 1943. We were at St. Jeans for just 18 days, and I was involved in just five flights; all practise formation. To our relief we were informed that we would be returning to the Western Desert again by the 1ˢᵗ September; to Derna this time. We learned much later that we were due to be part of an invading force to gain a foothold into the Balkans; Churchill described it: as 'a formidable force to push up through the `soft underbelly of Europe', i.e. The Balkans. Thank God this idea fell through.

Our `B' Flight Commander, Flt Lt Morgan informed Tom Chambers and I that he wanted us to collect two Spitfires from Bu Amud and deliver them to our next airfield at Derna. We were to set off on 27th August to make sure we arrived at Derna, with the two Spitfires, by 1st September. He said, 'you have three days to get there, so you should be able to spend at least a day in Cairo. Take your parachutes and small kit and make your own way to Bu Amud'. 'Marvellous!' Tom and I thought. So on 27th August we got a lift from St Jean to the main coastal road, ready for us to thumb a lift back to the desert area. Well, we just waited almost all day. There was hardly any traffic going eastwards and what there was wouldn't stop or wasn't going very far. Until, in desperation, the only thing that did stop was a horse-drawn cart with just one driver and a cartload of oranges, so we were glad to get aboard. The driver spoke some English and said we could eat as many oranges as we liked (we had two each). Well, the wretched horse and cart just lolloped slowly along, and we, of course, decided to get off. Luckily we were picked up soon after by an Army truck, which took us to the main airport at Tel Aviv. It was at the end of the first day and we were thankful to find a bed for the night and some food at the airport. Early next day we presented ourselves at the Control Tower and asked if there were any aircraft going to the Tobruk area. "Nothing to our knowledge" was the reply, until some American told us that across the airfield was a Liberator bomber that was getting ready to take-off for the Tunisian area - "they might be able to offer you a lift, but hurry up because they will be taking off shortly". So we literally ran around the airfield carrying our parachutes and small kit. The Liberator had two of its four engines running. We climbed aboard and found all the crew in the empty bomb-bay feverishly playing 'craps', all shouting and holding wads of notes. One of them spoke to us, asking what we wanted. We asked them if we could get a lift to Tobruk.

"Ask the Major (pilot), he's up front" was the reply. We did. "Yes," said the Major, "we can drop you off at El Adem. By the way, what's the crew doing? Are they still shouting and playing craps? Tell them I could do with some help up here!" Just after that we took-off and flew for several hours before landing at El Adem very late in the day. The crew were still shouting and playing craps as we got off the Liberator. They just waved 'cheerio' to us and off the bomber went, so to our knowledge none of the crew bothered to go up front with the Major.

We then had to grab a lift by truck to nearby Bu Amud, bed-down for the night and collect the two Spitfires the next morning. We flew them onto our new base at Derna where we rejoined the Squadron, feeling very tired and dirty after our escapade. So much for our day in Cairo!

The 3rd of September 1943 saw us operating again with scrambles and long convoy patrols protecting the lines of communication towards Malta and Italy. This routine continued but on the 19th the CO selected me, as 80 Squadron representative pilot, to attend the Middle East Central Gunnery School at El Ballah, situated by the Suez Canal in the Delta area. I was on No.6 Course and this comprised ten pilots drawn from squadrons all over the Middle East. The Course lasted for a month and was very interesting, with flying commencing on 20th September and continuing almost daily to 15th October. I flew 32 times and logged over 30 hours in the three types used on the Course – the Harvard II, Hurricane I and Spitfire VC. It was mostly air-to-air and air-to-ground firing, interspersed with cine-camera attacks, with the Harvard being used by the CO, Sqn Ldr Lyne, or other instructors, to assess us.

The CO of `A' Squadron was Flt Lt J.F. Edwards DFC, DFM, who was from North Battleford, Canada. He joined the RCAF in October 1940, and after training he was posted to the Middle East joining 216 Squadron in January 1942. This Squadron flew Bombay transport aircraft, but a few days later he was posted to 94 Squadron. He was at this stage a Sergeant Pilot, flying Kittyhawks. He destroyed a Bf 109 on

2nd March 1942 and another on the 23rd, and the following month he was posted to 260 Squadron, also flying Kittyhawks, having been promoted to Flight Sergeant. He claimed a probable Bf 109 on 15th September and on 21st October got a Macchi 202. Next day he shot-down a Bf 109, got a probable on the 26th and on the 28th destroyed one and probably a second. On 1st November he claimed a shared Bf 109 and on 30th December shot-down another and damaged a second. He was commissioned in November and became a Flight Commander in December. On 2nd January 1943 he shot-down a Bf 109 and on 8th April damaged a Fw 190. On the 15th he destroyed two Bf 109s and damaged a third, and on 22nd shot-down a six-engined Me323 transport aircraft. During those weeks he had received both a DFM and DFC, and in May his tour of operations expired. It was at this time that he became Flight Commander of `A' Squadron M.E. Central Gunnery School at El Ballah, by the Suez Canal, where I met him. All of the instructors at MECGS were experienced and successful fighter pilots.

After his time at the School, Edwards joined 417 Squadron, (November 1943), as a Flight Commander flying Spitfires, but the following month was posted to 94 Squadron. On 16th February 1944 he shot-down a Fw 190 and three days later claimed another and one damaged. The following month he was posted to Command 274 Squadron, and after leading the Squadron for a month in Italy he led the unit back to England. He flew a few sweeps over Europe and then when the Squadron began re-equipping with Tempests returned to Canada for a rest. He received a Bar to his DFC. In April 1945 he returned to Europe as a Wing Commander, and led No.127 Wing during the last weeks of the war. At the close of hostilities he had destroyed 15 ½ enemy aircraft, 14½ of them fighters. He also claimed 8 probables and 10 damaged and had destroyed over 200 motor vehicles. In July 1945 he became Wing Leader of No.126 Wing.

So ended a rather hectic four-week course at El Ballah - yet another airfield in the sand with tented accommodation, but this time situated right beside the Suez Canal.

It was always quite a strange sight to witness very large ships, and many naval vessels, travelling quite high out of the water, and gliding slowly by. My assessment at the end of the course, which was signed by Wg Cdr MacDonald, Officer Commanding, RAF Station, El Ballah on 15th October 1943 was:

1. *Marksman (air-to-air)*   *Average*
2. *Marksman (air-to-ground)*   *Average*
3. *Marksman (air combat)*   *Above Average*
4. *Instructor*   *Average*

Part of the reason for these courses was that the pilot who had been on the course could then pass on the latest 'gen' to the rest of the pilots in his squadron, but I don't recall being asked to pass on any of my new-found skills! No doubt the subject of the course came up in conversation in the Mess but that was probably about it.

I returned to dear old 80 Squadron, which had moved back to Savoia, in a Douglas DC-3 from Cairo West to El Adam; then by truck to Savoia. It was back to the usual stuff at Savoia - more convoy patrols, scrambles, and practise flights until the 4th of November when it was night-flying practise again. On one occasion I was coming into land and found it was taking far too long to touch down, finally ending up doing a mighty great loop at the end of the Goose-neck flare-path runway, and breaking the wretched Spitfire's undercarriage. The CO, 'Crash' Curry (remember, the NCO's friend!), was, I'm told, very disgusted and, I understand, was ready to banish me from his Squadron. However, I found out that the Duty Pilot had given me the wrong instruction for landing, which, unbeknown to me, meant I was to land 'downwind', which happened to be quite strong at the time. No wonder I couldn't get the aeroplane to touch down in time. I was able to report this on the Accident Form I had to fill in, and from that moment onwards heard no more about the incident. It was the first and only time I damaged an aeroplane.

On the 9th of November the Squadron moved to a place called Kabrit. I travelled in a Douglas DC-3, a journey of some 4 hours. We didn't stay long at Kabrit, which was near the Great Bitter Lake on the Suez Canal, near Suez. At Kabrit I flew twice on 16th November - cannon test and formation flying - but on 19th November we moved out again, flying from Kabrit to Heliopolis (45 minutes). The reason for the move to Heliopolis (Cairo Airport), which is by the Pyramids, was to provide air cover over the Allied Chiefs of Staff and Roosevelt and Churchill prior to them moving off to Yalta to link up with Stalin.

We returned to Kabrit on 13th December staying until 1st February 1944. Most of the time was taken up with practise bombing and much formation flying, with the ORB recording the main activity for this period as "practise bombing with live 500lb General Purpose bombs or 11½ lb practise bombs, along with squadron formation flying, battle flying and cine exercises. The 13th of January was the start of a series of exercises with the Navy in the Suez Canal, us providing top and bottom cover to intercept an attack by Beaufighters. R/T contact with Fighter Director ship was poor but intercepts were easy as the Beaufighters took no evasive action."

On the 9th of January I was able to claim I had been on the Squadron for one year. Then came the news we had all been waiting for - we were to move to Italy! I, for some reason, was one of those with no aircraft to fly so had to travel as passenger on a Douglas DC-3 in four stages over two days - Cairo West to Marble Arch, 5 hours 15 minutes - Marble Arch to Luqa (Malta), 3 hours 15 minutes - Luqa to Bari (Italy), 3 hours - Bari to Foggia, 45 minutes. Then it was by truck to Madna where I was reunited with the Squadron on 3rd February. The Squadron aircraft had arrived on 21st January and had started ops the following day, flying four offensive sweeps on 22nd January. By the end of the month 80 Squadron's score of enemy transport was 26 flamers. It was not until the first week of February that I was back with the Squadron and taking part in these sweeps.

On the 4th of February we carried out an offensive sweep over the Bomb Line. This entailed attacking trucks, guns, etc, which resulted in plenty of flak, but luckily no one was shot down. A very different game from the somewhat staid and boring convoy patrols!

The move to Italy involved operating from three different airfields (airstrips).

Madna – 3rd to 22nd February 1944

Canne – 22nd February 1944 to 13th March 1944

Trigno – 13th March 1944 to 4th April 1944

All these were quite near to the large cluster of USAAF airfields in the Foggia area of southern Italy. Madna and Canne were inland whilst Trigno was actually on the beach, with a single track of PSP running along the shore line. Great care was needed in both take-off and landing as the wind was invariably across the runway.

This was my first introduction into 'real' operational work as opposed to convoy patrols and 'readiness' spells, and I think most of us were really pleased to get our teeth into things. For me, I seemed to have been training and practicing for simply ages and felt well prepared for this more exciting insight into Squadron action.

Although the flak was invariably heavy when attacking vehicles and other MT, I felt that I could cope. In fact I almost enjoyed this type of work as opposed to escorting medium bombers, as it was the rather long flights over water to Yugoslavia that I did not much care for.

I flew again on the 8th of February, strafing in the Rieti and Sora area. On this op Flying Officer Holdsworth was hit by flak, but he baled out and although safe, was injured. The Squadron ORB recorded the mission: "Six aircraft offensive patrol Avezzano-Arsoli-Frosimone with one M/T destroyed (flamer) and one damaged. Flak

- intense inaccurate HAA at Alatri, moderate inaccurate LAA near Lake Cambrino, slight inaccurate HAA from Sora. Haze and low cloud met on outward journey had cleared by the time the aircraft returned. Fg Off R.S. Holdsworth (EP968) was seen to strafe the Frosimone-Ferrentine road but did not rejoin the formation. Some 10 minutes later he called ground station on Channel B saying that he was baling out. Nothing further was heard from him, he is presumed to have landed behind enemy lines."

On the 10th of February there was more strafing in Rieti area. I was one of four aircraft on the sortie and the Flight shot up motor transport, resulting in six flamers and five others damaged. Again plenty of flak but nobody hit. The ORB recorded: "four aircraft searched for MT reported snowbound at B9905 but nothing found. Continued on offensive patrol to Rieti-Rome road; in area Verola-Poggia two MT were attacked and damaged. A convoy of five trucks was attacked and four left flaming and one smoking. A second convoy of six 3-ton trucks was attacked; one left flaming, one smoking and one damaged. A large truck towing a trailer was set on fire." The latter part of February was fairly busy:

14th February – offensive sweep in Aquila area, but nothing was seen - 1 hour 35 minutes.

16th February - shipping recce just off the coast of Yugoslavia, Rogoznica and Split area -1 hour 45 minutes. The pair was led by Fg Off A.K. Ingle and we saw a trawler at the entrance to Split harbour, and a medium-sized MV (Merchant Vessel) at the pier in the harbour, but made no attacks.

On the 22nd of February another move: this time to a place called Canne.

24th February - more strafing in Rieti area - Flight able to destroy five vehicles, all flamers - 1 hour 55 minutes.

27th February - shipping recce to Yugoslavia, Zara area - small barge seen (we decided to leave it alone) - 2 hour trip (all over water!!).

29th February - shipping recce to Korcula and Zagorie area - another long, all over water trip - 2 hours 10 minutes - nothing seen.

March was a particularly busy month with the Squadron airborne most days; the ops I took part in were:

1st March - offensive sweep of Korcula, Yugoslavia - long trip again over sea, 2 hours 15 minutes - strafed small shipping. These sparse comments in my log book are given more detail by the ORB: "Six aircraft on anti-shipping strike. Three aircraft attacked along South coast of Korcula and South and North coasts of Peljesa peninsula and along the coasts of the mainland. At Lumbarda strikes observed on one 25ft boat, one one-masted schooner left smoking at Zuziana. At E8685 one 25ft boat set on fire. At Igrane two two-masted schooners attacked, one left smoking. One two-masted schooner at Podgora left listing. Three aircraft attacked North coast of Korcula. At Viganj small boat on beach damaged. At Orebic an armed motor launch left smoking. Intense accurate LAA at Lumbarda, one aircraft CAT II flak damage."

2nd March - strafe Rieti area, plenty of flak - 1 hour 50 minutes. Don Boyd missing, presumed killed. The six aircraft were led by Flt Lt G.N. Halliday, and I was flying my usual BR580. The ORB reported: "Six aircraft to attack railway targets on Avezzano-Rome railway, no targets seen. MT attacked on Rieti-Rome road; 10 MT destroyed, four damaged. As the aircraft set-course for base, glycol was seen to be leaking from one aircraft. Plt Off Boyd was heard to say that he would force-land. He was then at 500ft. He was called again on the R/T but made no reply and it is assumed that he landed about G0595." 'Crash' Curry went missing from a later op that day, shot down by flak. According to the ORB: "... was hit in the engine; he force-landed in the snow and reported by R/T that he was OK and was seen to get out of the aircraft and walk about." He survived the war as a PoW.

3rd March - strafe Termi to Rome road, 1 flamer and 1 damaged - 1 hour 50 minutes.

4th March - shipping recce in Hvar, Brac, Solta and Rogoznica area - another long flight over water to Yugoslavia coast - shot up a number of small boats - 2 hours 20 minutes.

11th March - weather and shipping recce, this time off the coast of Italy, Fabriano, Ancona and San Benedetto area - 1 hour 45 minutes.

Earlier this month, to replace our lost CO, Major D.H. Barlow, SAAF joined us as CO, and stayed with us until we returned to the United Kingdom in April. Major Barlow later became CO of 182 Typhoon Squadron, but was shot-down on 25th July 1944 by flak and was made PoW.

15th March - armed recce in Avezzano and Sora area. We had one SAAF Squadron as top cover to us, but nothing doing, weather dull - 1 hour.

18th *March* - armed recce in Yugoslavia Section, Rogoznica, Sibenik and Zara area, got 5 flamers - 2 hours, long sea trip! Again, the ORB adds more detail: "Six aircraft armed recce Rocozmica-Drmis area with two aircraft at 5,000ft and four aircraft at zero feet. Between U5366 and Drmis two 3-tonners with trailers destroyed, one 3-tonner and one staff-car destroyed. At U7877 one 3-tonner destroyed. At U7475 a loco with four open trucks attacked, strikes seen on loco and trucks. Moderate, accurate 20mm near Drmis."

20th March - armed recce in Termi, Rieti and Aquila area. Termi covered in cloud; we managed to destroy just one truck. One Squadron SAAF supplied top cover to us

- 1 hour 35 minutes.

21ˢᵗ March - armed recce in Yugoslavia after usual long sea trip - 2 hours 10 minutes, nothing seen.

22ⁿᵈ March - delousing for Baltimores at Popoli. 24 Baltimores bombed railway junction (we acted as top cover) - 1 hour.

24ᵗʰ March - strafe petrol dump at Gugliano-Wadi, well done over, but unable to observe much effect - 1 hour 15 minutes. This was recorded in the ORB as: "Six aircraft strafing petrol dump at Gugliamo. Gully strafed by all aircraft, smoke seen from gully but petrol dump obviously moved. No activity. One aircraft hit in coolant system, probably by small-arms fire. Engine seized over base and F/O Anderson crash-landed one mile from LG."

29ᵗʰ March - escort to 12 Kittyhawks as they bombed Spoleto - 1 hour 50 minutes.

31ˢᵗ March - escort to 12 Kittyhawks but target covered in cloud - 1 hour 35 minutes.

This was quite a hectic period on the beach at Trigno. The above operations were supplemented with long hours of readiness (sitting in cockpit), and waiting for scrambles, which usually never materialised. I remember one day a badly damaged USAAF Liberator, with at least two engines on fire or out, decided to crash-land on our PSP airstrip, ripping up most of the tracking as it skidded along on its belly. When we rushed over to it, the pilot (a Major I believe) climbed out unhurt and was laughing his head off. He said "I told them (his crew) I would get back in one piece, but they all jumped out over enemy lines - so now they must all be PoWs". He then lit up a big fat cigar. They had been bombing the Ploesti oil wells in Rumania and were based just south of us at the huge American airfields at Foggia. It took quite a time to clear our runway, which involved bulldozing the Lib out of the way, and then repairing the strip. Operating out of such strips was always tricky as you were rarely able to take-off or land into wind – there always seemed to be a cross-wind, which meant you had to be very careful; but as we were coming back as a four or eight to land in quick succession, you had to get it right. Once down in a three-pointer on the PSP you were OK, but anything else, especially with a cross-wind, and you were in trouble.

Memories of our short but hectic stay in Southern Italy will always remind me of the number of times we flew to the coast of Yugoslavia and back, involving quite a long time over the sea. The usual purpose was shipping strikes along this most beautiful coastline from Split, in and out of scores of small islands. We were instructed to shoot at anything moving. Well, when we came across small 'what looked like fishing vessels' we stayed clear; wouldn't imagine the enemy to be involved. Also the countryside and coastline of Eastern Italy, from Rimmini and places around, always looked very beautiful, but our job was to strafe motor vehicles on the coast roads, which we did, but there was always very heavy flak.

The end of March saw the Squadron preparing to leave the Italian scene and make ourselves ready to return to the United Kingdom to become part of the build-up to the invasion of Europe. The Squadron had started packing up on 1st April (an appropriate day?) for the move to the UK and the next day we flew our Spitfires from Trigno to Catania in Sicily, a journey of two hours, where we said a sad goodbye to our aircraft. We returned by transport aircraft to our base and on the 4th went by truck to Naples prior to boarding ship. The very day we arrived in Naples we were just in time to be met by an eruption of Vesuvius, with streams of lava pouring down some streets – a frightening and awe inspiring spectacle.

On the 10th we took ship (the HMS *Almanzara*) for home – a rotten old troop ship as I recall. The pilots were now well and truly separated for the voyage, with the NCO pilots to the bottom of the ship in some smelly hold, whilst the officers were given cabins and good messing facilities. The difference has always stuck in my throat. There would be much more of this segregation on main RAF Stations.

Operations over Europe

The ship docked at Gourock, Glasgow on the 21st and we were taken to our first airfield, Sawbridgeworth on 24th April. We were all struck by the simply beautiful GREEN countryside we passed through on our journey. Everywhere, the bright greens simply stood out - how lovely to be home again in such super countryside. We were immediately given 7 days leave, which was a bit mean after being overseas for nearly 2 years, although it was the same for others who had been away for much longer. So, still in our khaki battledress, we were off home and were told to expect a telegram telling us where to report in 7 days time. I was pleased to spend a happy 7 days at home at Wanstead with my mother, also visiting a number of friends and relatives, although my father was still at sea in the Merchant Navy. On the last day I received a telegram from the Air Ministry posting me to RAF Hornchurch, where I found the rest of 80, 229 and 274 Squadrons.

By the end of the first week of May, we were at the old Battle of Britain fighter station at Hornchurch, on the outskirts of London, where we were to reform as the Hornchurch Wing in No.11 Group Fighter Command. The new Wing Commander Flying was none-other than Wg Cdr E.P. Wells DSO, DFC and Bar, a New Zealander, and we were to soon become the Detling and the West Malling Wing. 'Hawkeye' Wells, as he was always known from the Battle of Britain days, had acquired the nickname 'Hawkeye' because he was considered by some to be the finest shot with the best eyesight in the Air Force. His final score was 13 destroyed. He moved on from being our Wing Commander Flying to command the Fighter Leader School - a truly super man. A Norwegian, Major Bjornstad DFC, was our new CO, and at long last, on the 9th May, our aircraft arrived – 19 Spitfire IXs. Local flying and familiarisation commenced the next day. We spent a hectic week at Hornchurch flying several times every day. Although our Spitfire IXs were not new they were much better than our old Mark VCs. We flew Wing and Squadron formation - just seven flights in all. On one occasion, taking off from our grass airfield, there were 12 aircraft at the same time spread right across the airfield. The CO was leading in the middle and I was on the right flank, and found by the time I became airborne I was almost going at right angles from the original line up - just scraping over the roof tops - a bit scary!

This is an appropriate time to reflect on the three fighters I had flown so far. Having flown the Hawker Hurricane for some 170 hours, it was a welcome change to find we were being equipped with the Spitfire Mark V, and all pilots were excited about the happening.

We found the Spitfire so much lighter than the Hurricane, and much more powerful and superior in take-off, climb, height and speed. On occasions, during mock dog-fights, the old Hurricane was a stronger aircraft, and if having to force-land, most pilots would prefer this aircraft. The Spitfire V was restricted in height, whereas the Mark IX with its 'blower' coming into effect around 10,000 ft was a major factor in any flying above that height. It also had a much higher ceiling. In other words, the Spitfire IX was a much better aircraft than the V.

On the 14th of May we flew a Wing Balbo, and it was always impressive to see such a large number of fighters in the air together; the following day was spent in bombing practise and on the 19th we moved 17 Spitfires to Detling in readiness for operations.

The grass airfield at Detling was on the top of Detling Common and the airfield was surrounded by a barbed-wire fence, which, I recall, was not very high. On sunny days, and on one weekend in particular (it could have been a Bank Holiday), a rather large crowd of people gathered just outside the fence. Many had driven their cars, and some had come on their bicycles. They had all come out on this perfect summer's day to have a picnic, and to just sit and watch our Spitfires taking-off and landing throughout the day. They would talk to us as we lounged in deckchairs outside our operations tents, either waiting to take-off or sitting around on readiness. Sometimes, if a Flight or Squadron of Spitfires landed and taxied over to our site, they would all clap and cheer - which was all rather embarrassing!

Apparently, it was what the local community liked doing on a sunny Sunday afternoon.

The Squadron was at 30-minutes readiness from the afternoon of 20th May, but it was the following day that the first op was flown, the CO leading eleven aircraft off at 0800hrs, with me in MH319. The route was Berck-Marle-Beaumont-Boulogne, but the weather was poor (low cloud), and we didn't find any targets worth attacking. We also had four aircraft return to based early with a variety of problems, which was not quite the start we had hoped for. The rest of May was taken up with bomber escort and the occasional sweep, although on 25th Warrant Officer Ross and myself were on standby when scrambled at 0455 to hunt for bogeys reported in the Hastings area. It was a fruitless search, and we landed back at Detling somewhat frustrated.

22nd May: top cover to Boston aircraft, which were bombing marshalling yards at Douai at 17000 feet. The ORB noted: "crossed French coast at 1956 and out at 2039, uneventful; slight very inaccurate medium anti-aircraft fire from Lille."

24th May - sweep - de-loused Evreux area for the withdrawal of the bombers - 1 hour 45 minutes.

I recall plenty of `readiness' each day, usually in the operations room or tent rather than sitting in our aircraft. There were usually four aircraft at readiness each day, from dawn to dusk as it were.

25ᵗʰ May: we were 'scrambled' to intercept 15+ bandits near Hastings. Nothing seen, and we patrolled off Dunkirk and Ostend area.

27ᵗʰ May: unusual experience. My Log Book indicates take off for *Ramrod* with 12 aircraft. I returned early (after 30 minutes) – 'kite u/s'. We were nearing Paris when I had a feeling that all was not well with my aircraft. My legs began to tremble, and I feared that I was 'chickening out'. I called the CO to say I was returning to base, as my engine was u/s. I flew back to Detling knowing that I had returned early, probably without due cause. However, as I was coming into land, there was a great puff of white smoke from the exhaust and the engine cut, and, of course, the propeller stopped. The Spitfire had suffered a massive glycol leak, and I was obliged to land 'dead stick' without damaging the aircraft. I was indeed praised for my efforts in getting the aircraft back in one piece - surely a premonition!

At the time, I recall, we were experiencing quite a number of problems with our rather ancient Spitfire IX's, and that on 10ᵗʰ June, whilst on a beachhead patrol, two of our pilots, Fg Off 'Jerry' Bush and Fg Off Larry Foubert RCAF, had to bale out into the sea, because of engine failure due to glycol leaks. Both pilots were picked up OK and uninjured. I noted that Fg Off Bush's aircraft, BS462, had been air tested by me twice on 28ᵗʰ May after engine trouble. Then on 19ᵗʰ June, Flt Lt Aylott from 274 Squadron, also based at Detling, went into the sea south of Beachy Head following glycol leak. He was on beachhead patrol, but was sadly killed. Despite this apparent problem with the aircraft, I do not recall anything being said or anything being done. However, something must have been done, as the Squadron records had this to say: "both pilots baled-out off Beachy Head because of glycol leaks possibly caused by the strain set- up by the 90-gallon long-range tanks." The entry for 11ᵗʰ June said: "most aircraft unserviceable whilst tests take place on the re-occurring problem of glycol leaks. The 90-gallon tanks are being replaced by 45-gallon tanks, which have proved adequate for beachhead patrols."

29th May - sweep *Ramrod* - 1 hour 35 minutes.
31st May - sweep *Ramrod* - 1 hour 30 minutes.

It was around this time, mid May 1944, that we first came in contact with the infamous 'Doodle Bugs' V-1s; several flew over Detling on their way to south London. Our Spitfire IXs were not fast enough to catch up with them, but I must say it was a very nasty new weapon and, as everybody experienced when the motor stopped, it was only a few minutes before the thing crashed and exploded. From spring of 1944, the Allied planners had been growing increasingly concerned over reports and air reconnaissance detailing a new German weapon that was being readied for launch against Southern England; one of Hitler's 'V' (revenge) weapons.

A considerable number of our operations were against these launching sites – referred to as '*Noball*' targets – some strafing, but mostly escorting the various bomber Groups attacking these sites: either the 'heavies' of Bomber Command (Lancaster and Halifax), or the 'mediums' of the Tactical Air Force (Mitchells and Bostons). For most of our stay in South England, starting on the night of 12th-13th June 1944 when the first of the V-1's were launched on England, records show that of the ten V-1's launched on that first night, only four actually fell on Southern England; there was a lull for three days while the Germans ironed out some minor difficulties. On 15-16th June nearly 250 flying bombs were despatched, of which about 140 crossed the English coast, and 73 reached Greater London. The V-2 rockets followed the V-1 flying bomb, and the first of those fell on Britain on 8th September 1944. Because of its supersonic speed there was no direct defence against it. The V-2 was a long-range fin-stabilized rocket weighing 13.6 tons on launching, and carrying a warhead of one ton of amatol and ammonium nitrate HE. Some 10,000 were produced, and between September 1944 and 29th March 1945, 1,115 V-2 rockets fell in England. A further 1,341 were aimed against Antwerp, and several others against Brussels, Paris, and Liege. Total casualties in England, from the total of 8,246 flying bombs actually launched, amounted to 6,139 people killed and 17,239 seriously injured.

D-DAY

The great build up to the invasion of Europe on 6th June (although we did not know the date at the time) was what had been engaging us for the past few weeks. There was no operational flying for us for the first 5 days of June. The Squadron ORB recorded that: "the standard was now 12 aircraft as part of a Wing with 229 and 274 squadrons; as might be expected, after 5th June, the Squadron was hardly ever released during daylight hours." On 5th June, to aid aircraft recognition, all our aircraft were painted with large white stripes on the top and bottom of the wings and part of the fuselage. So on 6th June, very early, we were all briefed for this tremendous event. The Wing was at readiness from 0430. Our job was to be part of the massive force of RAF and USAAF fighter aircraft that would cover the actual beachhead on `D-Day', and for a number of weeks to come.

The Squadron flew two missions on D-Day; the first involved two flights of four aircraft acting as cover for a convoy over North Foreland, with the first four airborne at 1100 and down at 1340, and the second four, with me as No.2, airborne at 1205 and down at 1355. It was exceptionally bad weather, and we didn't see much of the ships we were supposed to be patrolling and our patrol saw no action, but the earlier one had spotted a Ju.88 attempting to attack the ships and Fg Off Anderson had given chase, but with no result. The Squadron sent 12 Spitfires up at 1950 as escort to Albemarles towing gliders to St Aubin, with the fighters flying at 3-4,000ft; I was not on this op.

A similar shipping cover operation was carried out by the section I was in on 7th June, but this time it was over the beachhead. We were able to observe the truly enormous number of ships of all sorts, assembling off the Normandy coast. Many big ships - I recall the massive US Battleship `Mighty Mo' (the *Missouri*) with its huge guns belching out flame and smoke as it fired rounds off in the direction of

Normandy. It was possible to see where the shells landed with large explosions well into France, which was a truly memorable sight. We didn't see any enemy aircraft, but the massive number of Allied fighters over the beachhead, at their allocated levels, was very impressive. Our height was 18,000 feet. As usual, the Yanks wouldn't keep to their allotted altitude and were diving about all over the place and, at times, moving into our air space. I remember 'Spud' Spurdle firing warning shots in their direction whenever they came into our allotted air space.

8th June: weather very bad and the Wing returned early after 55 minutes.

11th June: more beachhead patrols - 1 hour 30 minutes. I flew as a pair with Fg Off Hanney on this convoy patrol (note: the Squadron ORB records the name as Harvey).

12th June: I was 13th man (reserve) when the Wing landed in France. The spare man or 13th 'bod' was to fly out with the Squadron almost to the target area, and if anyone had to return early for, say, engine failure, then the spare man replaced the one who was to return. No one fell out this time, so I returned to base, thus missing the opportunity of being one of the Squadron who landed on one of the makeshift airfields on the beachhead to await instructions, for the day. The Squadron landed at the St Croix R&R (Refuel and Re-arm) strip, and they returned to our base at the end of the day – pity I missed it!

The Wing didn't go back to France again during this period. I believe the airfields, just constructed, were too close to the enemy front and also huge clouds of dust were thrown up whenever the engines were started up, and the Germans immediately shelled the airfield - not a good thing!

13th June: another *Ramrod* - 1 hour 55 minutes escorting Bostons who bombed Caen - all seemed very accurate. Caen really looked a mess.

14ᵗʰ June: We actually came across enemy fighters! The Squadron had 12 Spitfires on a controlled sweep between Dieppe and Paris, and we were vectored by *Snackbar* to a group of bogeys half-way between Paris and Beauvais. We picked up seven or eight 109's and a single Fw190 and having jettisoned tanks, tipped over and dived at them. The enemy had seen us, and they half-rolled and spiralled down into the 6/10ths cloud layer at 12,000 feet before we could really get at them. I spent all of the time trying to keep up with the fellow in front of me, eventually losing him, and found myself going round in huge circles trying to get on the tail of one of the 109's. One flashed across in front of me. I gave it a quick burst with no effect, and then everyone seemed to disappear. I appeared to be on my own, so I put the nose down and returned to the U.K. at sea level, eventually catching up with another one of our Squadron, and together we landed at Detling. According to the Squadron ORB one Me109 was claimed as damaged by Fg Off Wiseman. We landed back at Detling at 12-30. Two more ops were flown the same day and I was on the last one, airborne at 20-30 to escort Mitchells from Selsey to Conde sur Vire.

15ᵗʰ June: two beachhead patrols - 2 hours 20 minutes and 2 hours 30 minutes.

18ᵗʰ June: shipping patrol - 1 hour 40 minutes. This was flown as the usual pair, and we had to fly at 2-3,000ft because of the hazy conditions, with the ships routing from North Foreland to Dungeness.

19ᵗʰ June: beachhead patrol - 2 hours 20 minutes.

21ˢᵗ June: Ramrod - Mitchells bombed *Noball* site at Abbeville - 1 hour 40 minutes.

22ⁿᵈ June: - another beach patrol, this time we landed at Tangmere - 2 hours 10 minutes. Later, again on 22nd June, we took-off from Tangmere for another beach patrol; this time landing back at Tangmere at night - 2 hours.

23rd June: we moved from Tangmere to Merston - 10 minutes. Merston was a satellite of Tangmere.

This constant moving around, although we didn't know it at the time, was a way of preparing us for this type of action when the Squadron's were eventually to operate on the Continent. So it was back to tents again, and all the discomforts that that entailed. We were at Merston for just 5 days, and I only flew a few sorties from here.

25th June: - another beach patrol - 2 hours.

26th June: - we flew to Tangmere - 10 minutes - and did two operations from there: escorting Dakotas to landing strips in the beachhead.

On the 28th of June we moved from Tangmere to Gatwick. The ground party had moved the previous day, as recorded in the ORB: "they arrived at 1900 hours and were greatly surprised by the ample messing and sleeping accommodation, although enthusiasm was somewhat damped by the news that there were very few cooks." Gatwick was just another grass airfield and it was more tents, unlike the massive commercial airport it is today.

1st July: escort Noball to St Martin Hortier, escorting Halifax bombers - 1 hour 30 minutes. The ORB recorded: "own height 17,000ft. Fairly intense heavy AA; area hidden by cloud, one bomber believed lost." Records show that a No.4 Group Halifax was lost on this op, which was one of three V-weapon targets attacked that day.

4th July: sweep. I was 13th 'bod' again, so no joy - 40 minutes.

5th July: Moved again, this time to West Malling; immediately we arrived we had to turn-round and set off on a sweep, but were almost immediately recalled.

6th July: escort and sweep - tackled some 109's but they wouldn't stay and just made off when they saw us - 2 hours 5 minutes.

According to the Squadron records, on 11th July, the CO called a meeting of pilots to discuss new tactics, but what I don't recall is that I was there, or what was discussed! A week later Major Bjornstad was posted to HQ Royal Norwegian Air Force and his place as CO was taken by promoting Flt Lt Spurdle to Acting Squadron Leader. From the operational point of view it remained as busy as ever.

12th July: escort Rouen area, Liberators escorted to bomb Noballs - 1 hour 35 minutes. Another sweep same day, but had to return early, `kite u/s'.

16th July: escort in the afternoon to Lancasters - 1 hour 10 minutes.

20th July: fighter sweep, again tried to jump 109's who wouldn't stay to fight - 1 hour 50 minutes.

25th July: Ramrod - Lancasters bomb airdrome near Paris - 2 hours

The 26th July 1944 was a different sort of day. Unbeknown to me, a cousin of mine, Peter Fisk, had visited an aunt of ours who lived at a nearby village, and she told him that I was stationed at West Malling. Peter was in the RAF as a Leading Aircraftsman. He arrived at the main gate, and asked if he could see me. The Station had a Tiger Moth aircraft for use by senior officers, and I got permission to take Peter up for a short spell of local flying. It was almost three years since I last flew a Tiger Moth, but was able to get it into the air, and we had an enjoyable flight around the local area. I was able to find our Aunt's small cottage in the village of Hadlow and we paid her an aerial visit, just avoiding blowing some washing off the line in her garden. We saw her waving to us as we flew over – at least I think she was waving! The trip lasted an hour and despite my unfamiliarity with the Tiger, I managed to land back in one piece at West Malling. I said goodbye to Peter, who I've never seen or heard of since, although I believe he survived the War and could still be alive. As always life is never as simple as it seems at first, and I was soon in conversation with the CO, Sqn Ldr 'Spud' Spurdle, who asked me if my cousin and I had enjoyed the trip. He then proceeded to ask if I knew anything about some very low-flying, as reports had reached the Station of an aircraft making low passes. I claimed innocence; I am sure he did not believe me but nothing more was said.

And so the invasion of Normandy was, at this stage, well underway and the various forces were steadily moving into France. These were certainly very hectic days. Our patrolling over the beachhead during 'D-Day', and the days that followed, were of intense interest - literally thousands of ships, many firing shells from mid-channel over the heads of the landing craft, to land well inside and beyond the coastal area. Also, on the rare clear weather days, there was a massive air armada patrolling the beachhead. There were literally thousands of fighter aircraft, many getting in each other's way. Each Wing and Squadron had its own allotted height to patrol in, at about 9,000 to 10,000 feet, and I must say that, all in all, it was a most memorable sight with all the shipping and air activity.

My log-book recorded another week of routine flying starting with a bomber escort on 28th July; a sortie lasting 1 hour 45 mins. The targets were a number of V-1 launching sites in the Pas de Calais and, in addition, the 159 Halifaxes were also supported by a small force of Stirlings and Mosquitoes. The weather was not good and bombs were dropped blind through cloud, although with apparently reasonable results. One Halifax failed to return, but we escort fighters had nothing to do as the Luftwaffe, as usual, was not in evidence. It was more of the same the following day with an escort to bombers over the Foret de Nieppe – a frequent target in the war against the flying bombs. I recorded this as cover for 60 Lancs, but the official account of the attack says that it comprised 76 aircraft, the majority of these being Halifaxes and with no Lancasters involved! After a few days with no flying for me, I

Dedicated to my wife Audrey (1921-1990)

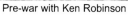

Pre-war with Ken Robinson

Post war with 'Tubby' Porter; Looe 1946

Year 1943		Aircraft		Pilot, or 1st Pilot	2nd Pilot, Pupil or Passenger	Duty (Including Results and Remarks)	Single-Engine Aircraft				
Month	Date	Type	No.				Day Dual	Day Pilot	Night Dual	Night Pilot	Day 1st Pilot
				—	—	Totals Brought Forward	58·50	67·45	2·20	2·35	
MARCH	24	D.H. 89A	7374	F/Lt. ASKEW	SELF	SECTOR RECCO.					
MARCH	25	MASTER I.	8767	F/O RIPPON	SELF.	DUAL LANDINGS.					
MARCH	25	HURRICANE I.	6622	SELF	"	3. FIRST SOLO. CIRCUITS.	0·25				
MARCH	25	HURRICANE I.	6622	SELF.	—	4. EXP. ON TYPE AND SECTOR RECCO		1·10			
MARCH	27	HURRICANE I.	6798	SELF.	"	CIRCUITS AND LANDINGS.		1·35			
MARCH	27	HURRICANE I.	7286	SELF.	"	5 D.F. HOMINGS. 10a CROSS COUNTRY		1·05			
MARCH	27	HURRICANE I.	6883	SELF	"	4. 10a		1·40			
MARCH	28	HURRICANE I.	1563	SELF.	"	7. FORMATION.		1·15			
MARCH	30	HURRICANE I.	1563	SELF.	"	7. FORMATION		1·30			
APRIL	1	HURRICANE I.	1563	SELF.	"	10B. 18 CLOUD FLYING.		0·45			
APRIL	1	HURRICANE I.	7068	SELF.	"	STEEP TURNS. FORCED LDGS 26.		1·40			
APRIL	1	HURRICANE I.	6798	SELF.	"	18a CLOUD FLYING 26 FORCED LDGS		1·15			
APRIL	2	HURRICANE I.	6798	SELF.	"	6. CLIMB 18000'		1·05			
APRIL	2	HURRICANE I.	6798	SELF.	"	CIRCUITS AND LANDINGS.		1·30			
APRIL	2	HURRICANE I.	6798	SELF.	"	20. CROSS COUNTRY (NAV. II)		0·10			
APRIL	10	HURRICANE I.	968	SELF.	"	18a CLOUD FLYING.		1·50			
APRIL	12	MASTER I.	9015	SGT. LEVINSON	SELF.	AIR-AIR AIR-GROUND DUAL		1·35			
APRIL	12	HURRICANE I.	6196	SELF.	"	12 AIR TO GROUND FIRING	0·45				
APRIL	12	HURRICANE I.	6803	SELF.	"	CAMERA ASTERN.		1·15			
APRIL	14	HURRICANE I.	1563	SELF	"	16 AEROBATICS.		1·00			
APRIL	14	HURRICANE I.	1563	SELF.	"	25a LOW FLYING SOLO		1·35			
APRIL	15	HURRICANE I.	3227	SELF.	"	7 FORMATION FLYING		1·30			
						21a SECTION ATTACKS 4000'					
						21b SECTION ATTACKS 12000'-15000'		1·45			
					GRAND TOTAL [Cols. (1) to (10)] 157 Hrs. 50 Min.	Totals Carried Forward	1·10 25·10 60·00	92·55	2·20	2·35	

Log Book extract for period at No.55 Operational Training Unit

Author in the 'office' of an 80 Squadron Hurricane

80 Squadron pilots on readiness at Bu Amud, early 1943: Left to Right: Bill Wise, Jock Stephen, Harry Ross, Stew Stewart, Billie Brown.

Middle East Central Gunnery School No .6 course, author standing 4th from Left

80 Squadron Hurricane IIC

ew recruit? Bf109 wearing 80 Squadron 'EY' code and RAF roundels

he Squadron also acquired a Ju87 Stuka

Bu Amud: author on Right

Bu Amud, March 1943 author with Len King

Chris House and 'Max'

The 'Pig' Period - an unflattering photo at Bu Amud plus a cartoon drawn by a 'colleague'.

Log Book extract February 1943, a typical month of operational sorties – mainly convoy patrols – and practice flying

Bu Amud February 1943, Stan Becks

Sqn Ldr David Jack

Bu Amud March 1943: Left to Right: Willy Wise, author, Chris House, Judy Garland, Len King, mess cook, Don Boyd, mess waiter; seated: Harry Ross, mess waiter

u Amud – the Jerry Jarrold birthday party with author centre stage looking the worse for wear!

eft to Right: Joe Preston, Don Boyd, Russ Foskett, Bob Smith, Billie Burke

The author poses for the camera; in the right-hand shot note the screwdriver – to puncture the Mae West if inflated in the cockpit

Harry Ross at Bu Amud in September 1943

...aving spent most of its time in the desert with Hurricanes, ...) Squadron re-equipped with Spitfires.

...ly, February 1944 with Harry Ross

80 Squadron,
West Malling, July 1944:

Sitting or standing on wing: WO Willie Williams, Fg Off Jerry Bush, Fg Off Nelson, Fg Off Murray Adams, Flt Lt Paddy Irish, Sqn Ldr Spud Spurdle, Fg Off Willie Wiltshire.

Standing: Fg Off Bill Preston, Fg Off Lofty Haw, Plt Off Harry Horsey, Flt Lt Gordon Milner, Fg Off Andy Anderson, Flt Lt Johnnie Heap, Author, Flt Lt Slim Burbridge.

Leaning on wing or kneeling: Capt Gillie Gilhaus, Fg Off Hugh Rorr, Plt Off Bluey Rankin, Plt Off Spike Maloney, Flt Lt Johnny Weston, Fg Off Larry Foubert.

YEAR 1944		AIRCRAFT		PILOT, OR 1ST PILOT	2ND PILOT, PUPIL OR PASSENGER	DUTY (INCLUDING RESULTS AND REMARKS)	
MONTH	DATE	Type	No.				
				—	—	—	TOTALS BROUGHT FORWARD
		X. Bob of EDMONTON.				SUMMARY FOR MAY, 1944 — UNIT 80 SQDN. — DATE 31·5·44 — SIGNATURE: Bill Gould	SPITFIRE IX " Offensive " Defensive
JUNE	6	SPITFIRE IX	MA 845 SELF	SELF X	—	98	SHIPPING PATROL
JUNE	7	SPITFIRE IX	MH 828	SELF	—	99	SHIPPING PATROL
JUNE	8	SPITFIRE IX	MA 845	SELF X	—		RAMROD. WEATHER DUFF.
JUNE	10	SPITFIRE IX	BS 462	SELF	—		AIR TEST
JUNE	11	SPITFIRE IX	MJ 281	SELF	—		AIR TEST
JUNE	11	SPITFIRE IX	MJ 311	SELF	—	100	SHIPPING PATROL
JUNE	12	SPITFIRE IX	MJ 311	SELF	—		13th MAN. No Joy !!
JUNE	13	SPITFIRE IX	MH 311	SELF	—	101	RAMROD.
JUNE	14	SPITFIRE IX	MJ 311	SELF	—	102	SWEEP.
JUNE	14	SPITFIRE IX	MJ 311	SELF	—	103	TARGET SUPPORT.
JUNE	15	SPITFIRE IX	BS 392	SELF	—	104	BEACH PATROL.
JUNE	15	SPITFIRE IX	BS 392	SELF	—	105	BEACH PATROL
JUNE	18	SPITFIRE IX	MH 878	SELF	—	106	SHIPPING PATROL
JUNE	19	SPITFIRE IX	BS 392	SELF	—	107	BEACH PATROL
JUNE	21	SPITFIRE IX	BS 392	SELF	—	108	RAMROD
JUNE	22	SPITFIRE IX	BS 392	SELF	—	109	BEACH PATROL
JUNE	22	SPITFIRE IX	BS 392	SELF	—	110	BEACH PATROL
JUNE	23	SPITFIRE IX	BS 512	SELF	—		MERSTON TO TANGMERE

GRAND TOTAL [Cols. (1) to (10)]
5.7.3 Hrs 30 Mins.   TOTALS CARRIED FORWARD

Typhoon IB – this is actually a 198 Squadron aircraft pictured in July 1944.

Log Book extract for June 1944, including a shipping patrol on D-Day

Typhoon cockpit

SERGEANTS MESS 124 WING B.L.A.

LÜBECK GERMANY MAY 1945

Menu

Celery Soup	Baked Potatoes
Fish Cutlets	Duchess Potatoes
Ravigote Sauce	Green Peas
	Braised Carrots
Roast Pork	Espagnol Sauce
Roast Beef	
Stuffing	Fruit Salad-Cream
Yorkshire Pudding	Cheese Straws

Wine & Beer

Pilot Daily Inspection card for Typhoon

Year 1945 Month / Date	AIRCRAFT Type	No.	Pilot, or 1st Pilot	2nd Pilot, Pupil or Passenger	DUTY (Including Results and Remarks)	SINGLE-ENGINE AIRCRAFT DAY Dual	Pilot	NIGHT Dual	Pilot	Remarks
					Totals Brought Forward	61.20	611.55	2.20	11.15	
	181	SQDN	HELMOND	B.86.						
	12H	WING								
MARCH 2	TYPHOON 1b	JP 835	SELF	-	SECTOR RECCO		0.50			
MARCH 3	TYPHOON 1b	JR 980	SELF	- 1	COVER TO 6 TIFFYS ON A/RECCE		1.05			COESFELD
MARCH 3	TYPHOON 1b	R7825	SELF	-	PRACTICE FORMATION		1.00			
MARCH 5	TYPHOON 1b	JR 266	SELF	-	A/RECCE. RETURNED EARLY		0.15			
MARCH 9	TYPHOON 1b	MN 990	SELF	- 2	COVER TO 6 TIFFYS ON A/RECCE		1.20			MUNSTER
MARCH 10	TYPHOON 1b	SW 403	SELF	-	PRACTICE FORM. & R.P. FIRING		1.00			
MARCH 11	TYPHOON 1b	SW 390	SELF	-	SPARE BOD!		0.10			
MARCH 12	TYPHOON 1b	PD 536	SELF	-	PRACTICE FORMATION		0.45			
MARCH 13	TYPHOON 1a	MN 950	SELF	-	PRACTICE R.P. FIRING		0.50			
MARCH 14	TYPHOON 1a	R7825	SELF	-	PRACTICE FORMATION		0.20			
MARCH 14	TYPHOON 1a	JR 337	SELF	-	SPARE ON OP.		0.15			
MARCH 15	TYPHOON 1b	SW 403	SELF	- 3	ARMED RECCE		1.05			S.MT. DEST.
MARCH 18	TYPHOON 1b	MN 990	SELF	- 4	ARMED RECCE		0.50			
MARCH 19	TYPHOON 1b	MN 990	SELF	-	PRACTICE R.P. FIRING		0.30			
MARCH 20	TYPHOON 1b	JR 265	SELF	-	PRACTICE R.P. FIRING		0.35			
MARCH 21	TYPHOON 1a	JR 265	SELF	- 5	ARMED RECCE. BURGSTEINFURT - COESFELD		1.10			RAIL TRUCKS, M
MARCH 22	TYPHOON 1a	JR 265	SELF	- 6	ARMED RECCE. MUNSTER AREA		1.00			RAIL TRUCKS S
MARCH 23	TYPHOON 1a	JR 265	SELF	- 7	ARMY SUPPORT TARGET - BOCHOLT AREA		0.50			5 BHT. GUNS
MARCH 24	TYPHOON 1b	JR 265	SELF	- 8	FLAK GUNS EAST OF RHINE		0.45			FLAK BATTERED
MARCH 25	TYPHOON 1a	SW 447	SELF	- 9	ARMED RECCE. AALTEN AREA		0.50			TANKS M.T.
				GRAND TOTAL [Cols. (1) to (10)] 702 Hrs. 15 Mins.	Totals Carried Forward	61.20	627.20	2.20	11.15	

Log Book extract March 1945

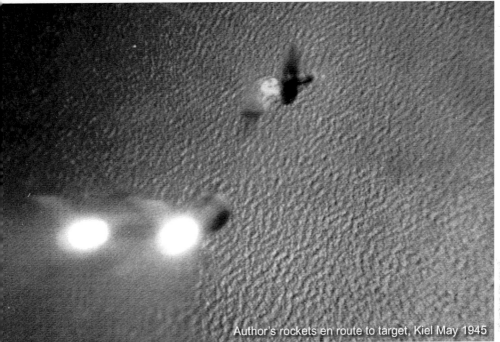

Author's rockets en route to target, Kiel May 1945

181 Squadron at Lubeck May 1945:
WO Bill Ironside, WO Syd Ainsley, Flt Lt Frank Sinclair, Sgt Gil Dawson, Fg Off Roy Cole, Sgt Bunny Austin, WO Des Desmond, WO Johnny King, WO Doc Milligan, Sgt ?, WO Harry Ash, Sgt Eric Boon, Fg Off ?, Plt Off Bob Gardner, Plt Off Phil Phillips, Fg Off Joe ?, Flt Lt Steve Stevens, Sqn Ldr Poppa Ambrose, Flt Lt Tommy Entwistle, Fg Off Pete Ballantine, Author, Fg Off Nobby Noble

No. 124 Wing NCOs' Mess, possibly Lubeck May 1945

Typhoon and Tempest Association reunion at Shoreham June 2001, author 5th from left

Spitfire talk with Carolyn Grace at Raydon

made two trips on 3rd August, a day when Bomber Command sent over 1,100 aircraft against various flying-bomb storage sites:

3rd August: target cover to Lancs bombing 10 miles north of Paris - 1 hour 50 mins. It was always impressive to see the massed ranks of bombers, and to watch the ground vanish in the mass of explosions as the tight concentration of bombs obliterated another patch of French countryside – and hopefully the V-weapons it contained.

3rd August: target support to Mitchells - 1 hour 34 mins.

4th August was a similar pattern and in addition to the bald statement in my log book "top-cover for Lancs – 1 hour 45 mins", I also commented that I had a "marvellous view of Paris." We were actually flying top cover to five squadrons of Spitfires, who were providing the close escort for the bombers.

5th August Just a short air test, then later in the day spare 'bod'; no-one fell out so I returned - 1 hour 45 mins. Having missed out on the mission, I spent the rest of day hopping in and out of Spitfires as I flew five more air tests, ranging from 15 minutes to 45 minutes, obviously with nothing worth noting, as my log-book makes no mention of any problems. Air tests were a regular feature of life on the Squadron, some were actually required by the groundcrew to check that a particular problem had been fixed, or as part of routine maintenance, and others were simply a good chance to get airborne on the pretext of a flight test.

7th August: looked like it might be a bit more interesting as we were on a fighter sweep in the Paris area, when ground control reported enemy aircraft in the area. Search as we might we found nothing, and the adrenaline calmed down again.

Two days later we were close escort to Mitchells bombing an ammunition dump in a wood near Rouen, with good bombing, but nothing for us. It was after we landed from this sortie that the CO told us that the Squadron was being re-equipped with Tempest Vs. This was met with mixed reactions as like most Spitfire pilots we had a definite affinity with the Spit; what made it even worse for me was that he told me that I was about to be tour-expired and that I would not be converting to the Tempest with the rest of the Squadron. This conversation had barely ended when four Tempests appeared in the circuit, broke and landed, then taxied to park near the control tower. This seemed too good a chance to miss, so I asked the Boss if I could have just one flight in a Tempest. There was a bit of 'discussion' but he eventually agreed, with dire warnings of what would happen to me if I dared bend the aircraft! With this authority and warning I cycled off to grab one of the ATA pilots who had delivered the aircraft to get a brief on how to fly it. In answer to my question as to 'book of rules' or Pilots Notes for the Tempest she – for like many ATA pilots this delivery had been made by lady pilots – said that no such publication was available, but that it was an easy aircraft to fly, not dissimilar to the Spitfire except that it was heavier and that it also had a tendency to swing a bit on take-off. That seemed to fulfil the Boss's requirement for a full brief from the pilot and so I was ready to go as soon as the aircraft had been refuelled.

It is hard for me to make any definite judgement on performance after just a short flight (I was airborne from 1400 to 1440 on a marvellous 40-minute flight in Tempest 'J'), but just to say that it almost immediately became apparent that the Hawker Tempest was going to be a fine aircraft to gradually replace the now aging Spitfire MkIX, and also any remaining MkVs.

My short flight told me that the speed was greater than the Spitfire IX and the overall climb was greater, but I'm not sure of maximum ceiling. However, as soon as they came into service, they were immediately put against the V1s and, I believe, they were the only Allied aircraft at the time able to catch up and destroy these weapons in level flight. In the short operational life with the RAF in World War Two, most were involved in ground attack, but with some air to air fighting, including the strafing of Me262 jet aircraft at their bases in Germany.

The Squadron ORB also noted the arrival of the Tempests:

"8th August: pilots attend a lecture by the Napier rep on the Sabre engine"

"9th August: 274 Squadron had some Tempests delivered, and we were able to borrow four of them for our pilots to fly. Everybody seemed very keen on this aircraft, although after so long the affection for the Spitfire is very strong, and most of the pilots are sorry that they are going off them."

11th August 1944 was my last flight with 80 Squadron and our Spitfire IXs; the mission was escort to 120 Lancasters attacking the marshalling yards at Douai, and I recorded it as 'wizard bombing'. The mission was 1 hour 40 minutes and on landing back at West Malling, I said many sad farewells. This mission was also given special note in the Squadron Operational Record Book, "this was the last time the two squadrons (80 and 274) flew together as a Wing under the old scheme of things. Unfortunately, two of the 274 Spitfires ran into each other on landing."

I had been with 80 Squadron for one year nine months from the Western Desert to Palestine and Italy, and finally, the UK and D-Day. I had flown 127 operations with the Squadron and amassed about 200-hours flying time. It had not been exciting in terms of combats or other drama but it had definitely had its moments, both humorous and tragic.

My spell with 80 Squadron whilst overseas was always at airfields, or more accurately landing grounds, with no buildings; we slept and lived and relaxed in tents. This also applied to Italy, but on return to the UK, we were billeted out in large houses, except our short stay at Gatwick, which was under cover. In the field (as it were) there was no segregation between messes, with all pilots, officers and NCO's using the same pilots mess, and thereby we had a very friendly and good relationship; this all stopped when we returned to UK, and was back to the old Officers and Sergeants Mess (except Gatwick).

80 Squadron	January 1943- August 194	
Period	**Aircraft**	**Main Airfield**
(18 Nov 1942)-Apr 1943	Hurricane IIC	Bu Amud (Note 1)
Apr 1943-15 May 1943	Spitfire VC	Bu Amud
15 May 1943-5 Jul 1943	Spitfire VC	Idku
5 Jul 1943-17 Aug 1943	Spitfire VC	Savoia
17 Aug 1943-3 Sep 1943	Spitfire VC	St Jean
3 Sep 1943-19 Oct 1943	Spitfire VC, Spitfire IX	Derna
19 Oct 1943-9 Nov 1943	Spitfire VC	Savoia
9 Nov 1943-20 Jan 1944	Spitfire VC	Kabrit
20 Jan 1944-23 Feb 1944	Spitfire VB & VC	Madna
23 Feb 1944-13 Mar 1944	Spitfire VB & VC	Canne
13 Mar 1944-2 Apr 1944	Spitfire VB &VC	Trigno
2 Apr 1944-10 Apr 1944	Spitfire VB &VC	Pottici & Catania
24 Apr 1944-5 May 1944	Spitfire IX	Sawbridgeworth
5-19 May 1944	Spitfire IX	Hornchurch
19 May 1944-22 Jun 1944	Spitfire IX	Detling
22-27 Jun 1944	Spitfire IX	Merston
27 Jun 1944-5 Jul 1944	Spitfire IX	Gatwick
5 Jul 1944-29 Aug 1944	Spitfire IX	West Malling
August 1944	Tempest	West Malling

Notes:

1. The Squadron had been at Bu Amud since November 1942, I joined them in January 1943.
2. Dates used here are based on official Squadron movement records.

I must say the Squadron spirit was much better when we shared the Mess. To a large extent it depended on the Commanding Officer, as 'Spud' Spurdle would always involve his NCO pilots in trips to the local pubs, and occasionally the beach for a swim. We all crowded on the Flight Commander's jeep or CO's vehicle and off we went. I recall returning to West Malling late one night with a large number of us all singing and shouting and hanging on the side of the jeep. We were going the wrong way round a roundabout and knocked the local village Police Constable off his bike! Fortunately, he was not too badly hurt and we bundled him and his damaged bike onto the jeep and took him back to the Mess and got him tight. I don't believe we ever heard anymore about the incident.

At other times when at Merston, in the Tangmere Sector, a number of us would go with the Boss in his car for a midnight swim in the sea at a place called Kings Beach, which I believe is quite near Bognor Regis, and we always seemed to make quite a lot of noise in so doing. It was just a case of 'letting off steam' I suppose.

With my last op flown with 80 Squadron, I was away on 1st September 1944, after a one week leave, to RAF Bicester in Oxfordshire. Before describing the latest posting, I would like to mention, and indeed list, the names and nationality of the many pilots I was privileged to serve alongside during years with 80 Squadron.
I served alongside 81 pilots from 9th January 1943 to 1st September 1944:

Nationality

British	38	New Zealand	3
Canadian	15	Norway	3
Australian	14	Irish	1
South African	5	Trinidad	1
		American	1

The Pilots

Fg Off 'Murray' Adams (Aus)
Fg Off 'Max' Aiken (British)
Fg Off 'Andy' Anderson (Aus)
Major Barlow (S.Africa), KIA
Wg Cdr 'Ron' Bary DSO, DFC (NZ), KIA
F/Sgt 'Stan' Becks (S. Africa)
Major 'B.J.' Bjounstad DFC (Norway)
Fg Off 'Don' Boyd (Aus)
W/O 'Stan' Brett (British)
Flt Lt 'Slim' Burbidge (British)

Flt Lt 'Billie' Burke (British)
Fg Off 'Jerry' Bush DFC (British)
Plt Off 'Billie' Brown (Canada)
W/O 'Frank' Calder (Aus), KIA
W/O 'Tom' Chambers (British)
Fg Off 'Col' Collingridge (British)
Fg Off 'Shorty' Compton (Canada)
Sqn Ldr 'Crash' Curry OBE, DFC (US)
Sgt 'Dave' Davidson (British)
Fg Off 'Jock' Findlay (British)
Sqn Ldr 'Rus' Foskett DFC (Aus),
Fg Off 'Larry' Fouber (Canada)

Flt Lt 'Ching' Friend DFC (British)
Flt Lt 'Judy' Garland DFC (Canada)
Lt 'Gilly' Gilhuus (Norway), KIA
W/O 'Pete' Godfrey (British), KIA
Fg Off 'Johnny' Haigh (British), KIA
Flt Lt 'George' Halliday (British)
Fg Off 'Barney' Handyside (Aus)
Fg Off 'Bob' Hanney (British), KIA
Fg Off 'Lofty' Haw (British), KIA
Sqn Ldr 'Johnny' Heap DFC (British), KIA
Major 'Dutchy' Henwick DFC (S. Africa)
Flt Lt 'J.D.' Hill (Aus)
Fg Off 'Stan' Holdsworth (Aus), Injured
Fg Off 'Bob' Holland (British), KIA
Flt Lt 'Chris' House (British)
Plt Off 'Dobin' Horsey (British), KIA
Sgt 'Joe' Hulse (British)
Fg Off 'Jock' Hunter (British)
Fg Off 'Alf' Ingle (British)
Flt Lt 'Paddy' Irish DFC (British)
Wg Cdr 'Jacko' Jack (British)
W/O 'Jerry' Jarrold (British)
Fg Off 'Len' King (British)
Fg Off 'Frank' Lang (Aus), KIA
Fg Off 'Mac' McCloy (Canada)
W/O 'Mac' McGregor (Canada)
Flt Lt 'Mac' McGregor (British)
F/Sgt 'Mac' McKay (Canada), KIA
Sqn Ldr 'Mac' McLachlan DFC (Canada)
Fg Off 'Mac' McLachlan (Aus)
F/Sgt 'Mac' McLachlan (Canada)
Fg Off 'Spike' Maloney (Aus), KIA
Flt Lt 'Gordon' Milne DFC (British)

Sqn Ldr 'Mitch' Mitchell DSO, DFC (British)
Flt Lt 'Morgy' Morgan (Canada)
Fg Off 'Wolf' Morris (British)
Fg Off 'Gus' Pratley (British)
Fg Off 'Joe' Preston (British)
Fg Off 'Bluey' Rankin (Aus), KIA
W/O 'Grem' Ross (Canada)
Fg Off 'Harry' Ross (British)
Flt Lt 'Tony' Seager DFC (S. Africa)
F/Sgt 'Shutts' Shuttleworth (Irish)
Fg Off 'Les' Smathers (Canada)
Flt Lt 'Bob' Smith DFC (S. Africa)
Flt Lt 'Smithy' Smith (Trinidad)
Sqn Ldr 'Spud' Spurdle DFC & Bar (NZ)
Fg Off Jock' Stephen (British)
F/Sgt 'Stew' Stewart (Canada)
W/O 'Streak' Swift (NZ)
Lt 'Ully' Ullstad (Norway), SD, Evaded
Flt Lt 'Phil' Ward (British)
Flt Lt 'Rollo' Waterhouse (British)
Sqn Ldr 'Ken' Watts (Aus), KIA
Wg Cdr 'Hawk-eye' Wells DSO, DFC (NZ)
Flt Lt 'Johnny' Weston (Canada), KIA
W/O 'Willy' Williams (Aus), KIA
Fg Off 'Willy' Wiltshire (British), SD, POW
F/Sgt 'Billy' Wise (British), KIA
Fg Off 'Dunc' Wiseman DFC (Canada)

Note: KIA – Killed in Action; SD – Shot-down;
Aus-Australian; S.African-South African; NZ-New Zealand

I think it was our New Zealand CO Sqn Ldr 'Spud' Spurdle DFC and Bar who commented on the very great strength RAF Squadrons possessed because of the varied nationalities of the pilots. They were from all over the old Empire and the Free World, plus those who escaped from Hitler's tyranny, as opposed to the pre-war RAF, when they were mostly university and so-called upper class types, with a smattering of NCO pilots usually re-mustering from ground crew posts. Although I was only to serve with 'Spud' Spurdle for a short period, he joined 80 Squadron at

RAF Hornchurch on 4th May 1944 as commander of the flight I was in (B Flight), so I got to know and respect him as a very experienced pilot. It was the beginning of his fifth tour of operations, and he was promoted to CO of 80 in July, serving until 4th January 1945.

The following is a short history of Spud's full operational tours in World War Two:

Unit	Dates	Comments
74 Sqn	20th April 1940 – 13th April 1941	
91 Sqn	15th April 1941 – 22nd May 1941	
MSFU	25th May 1941 – 20th Feb 1942	
91 Sqn	20th Feb 1942 – 27th August 1942	
116 Sqn	27th August 1942 – 24th Oct 1942	
2 FTS (RNZAF)	Jan 1943 – May 1943	CFI
16 Sqn (RNZAF)	25th May 1943 – Sept 1943	Solomons
80 Sqn	4th May 1944 – 4th Jan 1945	
Attached to Airborne Division 20th Feb 1945 –31st Mar 1945		
Attached to 114 Armoured Division 2nd April 1945 – 28th April 1945		

In all he flew a total of 564 sorties before being operationally grounded; he was truly a giant of a man and I feel honoured to have known and flown with him.

After I left the Squadron, I continued to communicate by letter with two of my closest friends in 80: Warrant Officer Pete Godfrey and Warrant Officer Harry Horsey. I must have written first to Pete, for I received a reply dated 5th September 1944 from the Squadron's latest base at RAF Manston, in Kent. The Squadron had moved there with its new Tempests at the end of August to be part of the V-1 defence system, as the Tempest had the performance to chase and catch the flying-bombs.

I must have replied to Pete's letter and it was not until a letter from my other good friend Harry Horsey dated 17th October 1944, telling me of the sad loss of Pete, and indeed many others I knew so well. Again, I must have replied to Harry's letter for

I received the second of his letters to me – this time dated 18th November 1944 and sent from Volkel in Holland. Volkel (airfield B80) was the Squadron's home from 7th October 1944 to 12th April 1945. I replied to the letter, but never heard again from Harry. Copies of the three letters are included at Appendix D.

At a much later date I learned that Harry Horsey had to make a forced-landing behind enemy lines and he was captured by the Dutch Police. Tragically, he was murdered by the German guards sent to collect him from the Dutch Police Station. It wasn't till many years later, around 1995, that Harry's nephew contacted me, and I got the full story. Appendix E contains material from Selhurst Grammar School, Book of Remembrance, and documents from the trial at Nurenberg of the two Germans who collected Harry from the Dutch Police and ending up killing him. A sad end to a fine colleague and friend.

REST PERIOD – 13 OTU

The posting to Bicester was meant as a rest tour from operational flying, and I joined the Fighter Affiliation element of No.13 Operational Training Unit on 1ˢᵗ September. The OTU had formed at Bicester in April 1940 with the original purpose of training light-bomber crews for No.2 Group of Bomber Command. In November 1943 it had transferred to Fighter Command and just after I arrived it had joined No.12 Group. We used Spitfire VCs for affiliation training and Martinet IIs for target-towing as part of the training course for crews destined for Boston, Mitchell, and Mosquito squadrons. The Chief Instructor was Wg Cdr E.D. Crew DSO, DFC and Bar, a very experienced fighter pilot with 15 confirmed victories over enemy aircraft, plus an impressive tally of V-1s.

Two days after arriving I flew my first details, a local area flight in the Martinet II, (with a winch operator in the back), for familiarisation with the area and the aircraft, plus practise drogue release, and including towing a drogue target for Bostons.

This type of flying was interspersed with the rather more enjoyable trips in one of the small number of Spitfire Vs that were used for fighter affiliation. This could involve up to six Mitchells or Bostons with the Spitfire making dummy attacks on the formations, so that the formation could practise it self-defence tactics. The attacks were filmed, as was the 'gunnery' from the bombers, and all agreed that this was invaluable training. Equally important were attacks on single aircraft, as this allowed the crew to practise their evasion tactics, and some of those bomber pilots really threw their aircraft around. A typical day might involve four or five target-towing flights in the Martinet, and with the odd fighter-affiliation trip as well, it was certainly a busy period. Like all OTUs ours was a very busy one, and because of that it used a number of satellite airfields, such as Finmere, Chipping Warden, and Hampstead Norris, as well as other airfields on an 'as required' basis; this usually being the case when certain training areas or ranges were programmed.

On one of my flights I was accompanied an LAC whose job it was to release the winch and let the drogue target out. Very shortly afterwards I saw gunfire very very close, and upon enquiring was told by the LAC that the winch was stuck and only a few feet of cable had reeled out with the target. I told him in no uncertain terms to cut the cable and this he eventually did with his penknife, but far too slowly for my liking. On coming in to land, the unfortunate and very scared LAC leapt out of the aircraft, was promptly sick, and then disappeared never to be seen again! (Note: Jerry is unsure of the location of this incident, although the memory if the event is vivid. It may have occurred during his short time with 695 Squadron at the end of the war).

In mid October the OTU moved to Harwell, but the training routine remained the same, and I remember using the satellite airfields and other locations such as Grove, Woodley and Weston Zoyland, the latter when we were using the range areas over the Bristol Channel. We had an average of four or five Martinets and four or five Spitfires, and a limited number of pilots for them, hence the fact that I was kept busy throughout October and November.

Life at the OTU was OK, but after squadron life it was all a bit dull and the social life was virtually non-existent in comparison. I was able to get a few weeks leave from 11th December, with instructions to "to report back to Harwell at 2359 hrs on the 29th December." This meant I could go home for a decent break, and I spent a very pleasant couple of weeks with my mother who was living in a small village called Wateringbury near Maidstone in Kent with her sister, as our house in Wanstead had been bomb damaged some time previously. I was very happy, indeed delighted, to meet up again with my father, who I had last seen when he and my mother saw me off in London when I was to report to RAF Cardington to start my time in the RAF in early 1940. My father and I had lots to talk about, and I recall asking him about a certain Atlantic convoy known as the Jervis Bay Convoy (officially Convoy HX84), when a German battleship (*Admiral Scheer*) had attacked a convoy of ships in mid Atlantic consisting of some 38 merchant ships, which had only one escort, the merchant ship HMS *Jervis Bay*. This had been converted into an armed merchant cruiser and manned by 290 Navy personnel under the command of a Captain Fegen. The *Jervis Bay* scattered smoke floats and sailed into the battleship, ordering the convoy to scatter – the *Jervis Bay* was sunk with most of her crew. Captain Fegen was amongst the casualties when the bridge was hit and was awarded a posthumous VC. The gallant action of the *Jervis Bay* saved much of the convoy, as the 24-minute one-sided battle allowed the convoy to scatter into the approaching darkness; only five merchant ships were sunk, the rest scattered – half back to Halifax, Nova Scotia, and the remainder to Liverpool.

I told my father that I had heard about the action that had occurred in mid Atlantic, and was given time off to proceed to Liverpool in the hope of finding the *Pacific Enterprise* (Dad's ship, of which he was Chief Engineer). News of the action had named quite a number of the merchant ships involved and included the *Pacific Enterprise*. I arrived at Liverpool and rode the elevated railway, which ran alongside the miles of docks in Liverpool. But try as I may, I was not able to trace my father's ship, and I eventually gave up and returned to base. It was at this Christmas meeting that my father was able to say that his ship was one of those that had returned to Nova Scotia. He had tremendous praise for the merchant cruiser that kept the German warship at bay – long enough for most of the convoy to get clear.

I ended up catching the last possible train to get to, I think, Newbury Station, in time to catch the connecting train to near Harwell, along with many of my RAF colleagues also returning from Christmas leave. It happened to be a brilliant star-studded night with a deep frost on the ground and quite a number of us had to walk quite a way across the frosty fields to reach the camp, with the main topic of discussion being the loss of Glen Miller. The news had just come through that Glen Miller, the famous American band leader, had gone missing whilst flying across the North Sea to somewhere in Europe. At the time there were many stories of espionage activity by Miller and that he was killed on some cloak and dagger mission. To this day there has been speculation that his plane did not crash into the North Sea as was given out to all authorities. Whatever may have occurred, he was a great loss to all the many millions who enjoyed his style of music, and this memory lives on in a great many bands that still play his music. 'Glen Miller' evenings are still popular; the airfield from which he left – Twinwood Farm – now has a museum located in and around the control tower and the museum occasionally holds Glen Miller dances.

In all I flew 26 hours on Spitfire IIs and VCs, 32 hours on Martinet Is, with mostly three or four flights on each of the flying days. I found it quite interesting, but I was keen to get back into an operational squadron.

Rest tours were always intended as a short break from operational flying, and after a final, and enjoyable, day of three fighter affiliations in the Spitfire, I said farewell to Harwell.

SECOND TOUR – No. 181 SQUADRON

I was ordered to report to No.83 Group Support Unit (GSU) at Tangmere, although when I arrived I discovered that the unit was in the process of moving to Dunsfold, near Godalming in Surrey – a move that had started in November. I duly caught up with the GSU on 7th January and was soon learning to fly my third RAF operational type, the Typhoon. The GSU had been established in March 1944 to maintain an immediately available reserve of trained pilots for the squadrons of No.83 Group in order to provide replacement pilots and aircraft for the Group's squadrons. This meant taking on the operational training of pilots, but not initially the conversion to type, although by the time I arrived the unit was also acting as a Typhoon I conversion unit. Losses amongst the squadrons had been heavy since the invasion in June, and as the Tactical Air Force moved through Europe the ground-attack squadrons continued to suffer significant losses to the effective German light anti-aircraft fire.

I started flying on 21st January and completed the course by the 25th February 1945; this comprised some 17 flights in the Typhoons, with familiarisation on type, local flying, low flying, formation, dog-fights, low flying and map reading, together with cannon firing and the use of rocket-projectiles (RPs). There, of course, is no dual control in the Typhoon; you just studied the Pilots Notes, sat in the cockpit and off you went. I found, after the Spitfire, that the Typhoon was quite a bit heavier, but after a dozen or so flights, I, and in fact we all, thought the Typhoon was a splendid aircraft and we couldn't wait to get onto a squadron. It was a difficult aircraft to take-off because of the torque from its powerful engine and you had to be very careful; it was invariably a spot of fiddle-assing with the rudders and being ready to catch any swing, for as soon as you put on the power and released the brakes you had to correct the swing right away, especially if the wind was not down the strip.

One incident occurred, as I remember, when I was enjoying some local flying at about 10,000 ft on a beautifully clear sunny no-cloud day, just inland from the seaside town of Bournemouth. I was happily flying along straight and level, – when suddenly all around me appeared large puffs of black smoke – 'soot bags' we called them – flak – anti-aircraft shells bursting. I immediately took evasive action, half rolled over and dived down to ground level and hurried back to base at Dunsfold. I recall looking down on the outskirts of Bournemouth and saw much activity from some gun emplacements. On return to Dunsfold, I put in an immediate complaint, and it wasn't long before the sector people came back with the news that an American anti-aircraft battery on the outskirts of Bournemouth claimed they had damaged a Fw190, which was typical of that trigger-happy lot – lousy aircraft recognition!

On 26th February 1945 I found myself posted to 181 Squadron in Holland.

Ground Attack with RPs and Cannon – 181 Squadron

On the 28th of February 1945 I arrived at RAF landing strip B86, at a place called Helmond in Holland, and, I believe, I travelled from Dunsfold by Anson aircraft: I was now a member of 181 Squadron equipped with the Hawker Typhoon IB.

Helmond (B86) was just a short airstrip carved out of a very muddy field alongside the main road to Eindhoven. The narrow runway (the only one) was constructed of PSP (Pierced Steel Planking). We were billeted in a rather austere looking 4-5 story barrack-like place, which happened to be a monastery, and the monks and their pigs and other animals now occupied the ground floor and basement, and we, the RAF, had the upstairs rooms for eating, sleeping, and 'drinking'. The Squadron had been flying Typhoons since September 1942, and had been amongst the first RAF squadrons to move to France, hopping from Merston to B6 (Coulombs) on 20th June 1944, only two weeks after the Normandy landings. Helmond was their sixth base on the Continent and they had been there since 3rd February, having spent much of

January at Warmwell on refresher training for RP work. My arrival was noted in the Squadron Record Book – not that I saw it at the time: "Another pilot rolled in today – Fg Off P.S. Ballantine – and later, another, W/O C.W. Jarrold. Both are second-tour blokes and we wish them a happy and successful stay with the Squadron."

I reported to the CO of 181 Squadron the day I arrived. S/L 'Poppa' Ambrose DFC and Bar was another of those great wartime characters, and 'Poppa', as he insisted he was to be called by his pilots, and not SIR or BOSS, was a great guy and told me that he had been in Typhoons all his operational time and this was his fourth tour. He also said he had been a Sergeant Pilot and that he was pleased to have a very experienced pilot (me) posted to his Squadron. He wanted to know why I hadn't been commissioned, as I was a Warrant Officer at the time, and he certainly made me feel welcome. He also said he would recommend me for a commission in a short time.

So started my second tour of operation. I had one short 'famil' flight – a sector reconnaissance – on 2nd March. That same day the Wing undertook practise flying and a dummy attack; this was recorded by the Squadron diarist: "We Penguins were treated to the grand spectacle of a dummy attack on Flying Control by the whole Wing. It was an impressive sight, and we felt a great amount of satisfaction in imagining what the Square-Heads must feel like at the receiving end of such an attack, and especially with the addition of screaming rockets."

The next day I was back in action providing cover to six Typhoons on an armed recce in the Coesfeld–Haltern area, but also with freedom to attack targets. The result was one locomotive and seven MT claimed by our flight – a quite exhilarating start to this new tour. This was the bread-and-butter of what we did, as everything that moved on rail and road on the German side of the road was fair game, and this disruption of transportation was a key part of the Allied strategy; it was particularly important to destroy locomotives, as much of the German military material was moved by rail, and locos were one of the weak points in the system as they were in short supply.

I was allocated to 'A' Flight under Flt Lt 'Dizzy' Compton DFC, who was shortly to be transferred to become a Flight Commander in one of our sister squadrons (182 Squadron), and his place was taken over by Flt Lt John Derry. This fine pilot later became a test pilot, but sadly lost his life at the 1952 Farnborough Air Show whilst displaying one of the prototypes of the DH110 (Sea Vixen).

We were one of four Typhoon squadrons in No.124 Wing of the 2nd Tactical Air Force, and from this period to the end of hostilities on 7th May 1945, these four Squadrons, 137, 181, 182, and 247, mostly operated from the same airfield, but sometimes, because of constant movement and size of airfield, they were occasionally based in different airfields. The Wing was commanded by Gp Capt Eric Bitmead DFC, with Wg Cdr 'Kit' North-Lewis DSO DFC as Wing Commander Flying, and the four squadrons were commanded by Sqn Ldr R. G.C. Barraclough (137 Sqn), Sqn Ldr 'Poppa' Ambrose DFC and Bar (181 Sqn), Sqn Ldr C.J. Grey (182 Sqn), and Sqn Ldr J.H. Bryant DFC (247 Sqn).

Life at Helmond was extremely hectic with really not too much time for relaxation as most of the day was divided between flying or readiness and was mostly spent in what was called the Pilots Equipment Room. Our kit and parachutes were kept here also, with the 'readiness' and 'ops' board also being located in the Room. There were plenty of chairs to loll about on whilst waiting for flying, or a truck to take us back to the Mess at the monastery up the road. The hut was well heated by big coal and wood-burning stoves.

Flt Lt 'Frankie' Galbraith, a Canadian, was sadly killed on 5th April after being shot down by flak on an armed recce operation in the Rhine-Lingen area. Frankie was a super guy – I remember he had recently received a large birthday cake from his mother in Canada and as usual every pilot was given a piece. It must have been just after his birthday that he was killed.

We did manage to make quite a number of trips into the local town of Helmond. On one occasion the Squadron pilots were invited to attend a dance in the village hall and most of us agreed to go. I, and several of my new pilot colleagues attended, and spent most of the time drinking at the bar rather than dancing (I've never really mastered the art of dancing!), and when it came to the going home time, three of us missed the last truck back to the airfield. I was quite worried for I was 'on readiness duty' at dawn next morning, and it was important to get back. A message came back from my Flight Commander, John Derry that he would send the truck back for us and not to worry. The truck duly arrived and we got back to camp OK. The following morning, feeling rather 'under the weather', I discovered that I had overslept – the orderly had not wakened me, and I missed my 'readiness' duty – a quite serious offence. It turned out that John Derry did my 'readiness' stint for me and had arranged for me <u>not</u> to be awakened by the orderly. We all thought that was a magnificent gesture by our very popular Flight Commander, who later in the month left 181 Squadron to become the CO of 182 Squadron and was promoted to Squadron Leader – a superb character liked and respected by all.

On another occasion our Squadron was challenged by an Army team to play them at football in the town's (Helmond) football ground. I was amongst those selected to play – at Left Half, I seem to remember. We only played 20 minutes each way, as most of us were too unfit for a full 90 minutes! The Army side had several professional footballers in their team and we were thoroughly beaten. I was absolutely shattered by the running around part – as were all the RAF team.

The flying was quite intense at Helmond, and I was involved in some fifteen operations in the period 3rd March to 10th April including:

3rd March: Cover to six Typhoons on armed recce in the COESFELD – HALTERN area. Our flight of four destroyed one loco and seven MT (motor transport) – 1 hr 5 mins.

9th March: Again cover to six Typhoons on armed recce – MUNSTER – BURGSTEINFURT area – 1 hr 20 mins.

15th March: Armed recce – BURGSTEINFURT – COESFELD area - we destroyed five MT.

18th March: Armed recce – 50 mins.

21st March: Armed recce – BURGSTEINFURT – COESFELD area – we hit rail trucks and MT. Also shot up rail lines leaving large gaps in track – 1 hr 10 mins.

22nd March: Armed recce – MUNSTER area – rail tracks shot up causing rail cuts – 1 hr. According to the ORB six trucks were destroyed and six damaged, along with the cut in the railway at A7376.

23rd March: Army Support Target – BOCHOLT area – this type of operation was called 'CAB RANK' – Army laid down white smoke on the target and we came down and destroyed them by rocket and cannon fire – this time 88mm guns and a house well pranged - 50 mins. "All RPs went into the target, which included a house, and good results were seen" (ORB).

The Rhine Crossing Operation

24th March: Rhine Crossing with more Cab Rank targets. Flak guns pranged for Airborne Landings – Wg Cdr North-Lewis shot down and 'Missing', but evaded – 45 mins. This was a busy day for 181 Squadron with six anti-flak patrols flown from

0930 to 1915; four as 4-ships and the last two as 6-ships. I only flew on the first of these, led by 'Poppa' Ambrose, who went on to fly twice more that day.

The Rhine Crossing was the last major combined Army, Air Force, and Parachute battle in World War Two, and I well remember the simply massive air armada, which seemed to form directly overhead our airstrip. The sky for the first day was simply filled with aircraft towing gliders – most Douglas C-47s (Dakotas) – but there were also many other glider towing or parachute aircraft going into the Rhine area. The flak was intense and many aircraft were damaged by the tremendous firepower of the German guns. As we were close to the action some tried to crash-land on our airstrip, but most flew on (some on fire) overhead. It was a very hectic few days.

April saw most of us flying most days – usually Armed Recces or Army Support Target – where tank, guns and MT vehicles were shot up or rocketed for the Army. Cab Rank operations usually consisted of four Typhoon aircraft in a finger-four formation, flying somewhere near the so called 'bomb line' below the cloud level – usually between 8,000ft and 10,000ft – patrolling a certain area prescribed by the RAF Controller (Radio) who was attached to the Army. The Army would tell the controller the position and type of target; for example a number of Tiger tanks hiding in a wooded area, and they would mark the spot by launching a white smoke shell to burst over the said spot. The RAF controller contacted us with the details and the leader would get us into position and when we saw the smoke we would wing-over and dive down on the target and release a salvo of rockets and/or cannon fire. Usually, we were welcomed by an intensive flak barrage, and it was not a very healthy place to be – especially if we had to go round again!!

It was on the actual day of the Rhine Landing Operation that our Wing Commander was shot down by flak when he led an attack on a defended strong-point at Krudenburg to the East of Wesel in support of the crossing of the Rhine by the 2nd British Army, which had been launched at dawn that day. After diving from about 12,000ft his

Typhoon was hit as he was pulling out, and he immediately set off for the Rhine to try and make the British Lines. Unfortunately, when over Wesel the engine stopped, and he had to crash land on the first open space he could see. He made an almost perfect wheels-up crash landing and came to rest on Gravel Island just to the north of Wesel. Upon climbing out of the aircraft, he found he had landed a few hundred yards from a German Parachute Regiment manning trenches on the banks of the Rhine.

A German paratrooper shouted something to him, and without more ado he put his hands up. He was taken along trenches (which were quite extensive, and had a field of fire across the Rhine), and led to the Command Post of the German Company Commander. He stayed here all day, but, unfortunately, they had no food, so they remained hungry for the whole of his stay. That evening, after a day in which these particular Germans were not engaged, the Commander intimated that Wg Cdr North-Lewis was to be sent to his Battalion HQ under escort, but, they learned they were cut off, as British paratroops had landed to the East of the position. The Commander then intimated that if his position did not change he would surrender the next morning.

The Wingco was much relieved, as it seemed he should soon be back with our side. However, during the night, he was woken by a sudden disturbance when another officer arrived. He was a most determined looking man with a mass of decorations including the Iron Cross, with a large scar on his face, and stick grenades in his belt. He obviously wanted to break out and to take the Wing Commander with him! Fortunately, after a heated exchange, the other officer prevailed and the stranger departed. At dawn on the 25th, the Wingco began to wonder how he could get back. Then, around 8 a.m., a British artillery-spotter light aircraft flew over and he managed to attract its attention. He requisitioned a number of German towels and tore them into strips and laid them out to read 'Have Hun prisoners – send help'. But although the plane acknowledged, he had no idea when help would arrive. Meanwhile, he was shown around and it was then that he spotted a canoe complete with paddle. Although he had never paddled before, he decided to use it, and the Germans carried it down to the Rhine.

He then set off across the river, hoping the Germans would not shoot from the back, nor the British from the front. Nearing the British side he could see troops in a firing position as he took out his handkerchief and shouted 'Don't shoot, I'm a British Officer'. The troops were from the Highland Regiment, but their main interest was in the prospect of loot! 'Had the Germans any watches?' he was asked. He was quickly taken to Brigade HQ and given a meal. He saw the Divisional Commander and was then flown back by light aircraft to our base at Helmond. Here, he was greeted by Air Vice Marshal Harry Broadhurst, who informed him that he had been awarded an immediate DSO, and he also forbade him to fly on operations again for some time.

25th March: Armed Recce – Isselburg-Aalten area, tanks, MT and staff car shot up by us - 50 mins. The official result was two tanks destroyed and two damaged near Bocholt, plus seven MT destroyed and one damaged.

26th March: Army Support target – shot up guns in wood - 35 mins. It was another busy day for the boys as 181 flew 32 sorties in four ops "comprising three sections of six on armed recces, a six attacking gun positions and a ten making an attack on a wood in which there were Huns and guns." (ORB)

28th March: Armed Recce – and more Cab Rank stuff – 1 hr 5 mins.

On 31st March my very good friend Warrant Officer Syd Ainsley was shot down by flak near Enschede – he was one of four Typhoons carrying out Army Support. He was hit by flak after pulling away from the target, and reported to his leader that he was hit and would have to force-land. The problem was, which side of the 'bomb line' was he on? The Flight Leader sent the other two aircraft back to base, while he decided to circle over the position where Syd had crash-landed. I learnt afterwards from Syd that it was in fact just over the bomb line on <u>our</u> side, and as he got out he was soon confronted by a farmer and his family, and they all wanted to shake his hand and pat him on the back!

Syd was entertained in the farm house with food and drink until he was collected by the local police. Unfortunately, the Flight Commander above thought differently and when he landed back at base, reported that he thought Syd had been stabbed in the back by Germans and was probably killed. In fact Syd was made most welcome and handed over to some British Army personnel. He was greeted by the Army Major who took him into the Officers Mess (in some building or other) and said he could stay the night and take food there, but they were all pulling-out during the night and he would be left with a jeep and driver to take him back to his RAF base. The Major asked him what had happened to the gunner and navigator in the Typhoon, as he couldn't understand how just one person flew and navigated and fired the guns and rockets at the same time! Anyway, next morning he found all the troops had left – except for a jeep and driver to take him back to the RAF. Syd arrived back at Helmond looking very tired, unshaven and feeling rather low. I always remember him telling me that he reported to our CO, Sqn Ldr Ambrose, who at first said he was pleased to see him back on one piece, but then went on to 'tear him off a strip' for 'taking someone else's parachute', and that he'd 'better get back in the air, so that he wouldn't dwell on the shooting down. So Syd, feeling rather crestfallen by the parachute 'strip-off', took the first Typhoon requiring an air test.

Speaking to Syd, many years after the event, he said that one of the main things he always remembered was the fact that I had saved him a piece of my recent birthday cake! I kept in touch with Syd over the years, meeting up with him on a few occasions over recent years, and always speaking on the telephone a couple of times a year.

3ʳᵈ April: Armed Recce – LINGEN area - 1 hr 10 mins. Visibility was poor and we didn't find anything to attack.

5ᵗʰ April: Armed Recce – REINE – LINGEN area – 1 hr 30 mins.

7ᵗʰ April: Army Support Target – LESSE on river WESER – cab rank – Railway station pranged – 1 hr 45 mins. The ORB stated: "Lesse a marshalling yard, in which there were 30-50 trucks was attacked. All RP went into the target but no results were seen. Ground control reported good results."

During three days of bad weather (8-10ᵗʰ April) the opportunity was taken for a spot of football, as recorded in the Squadron ORB: "9ᵗʰ April A Flight v B Flight, this time the activities of a referee were dispensed with altogether. A Flight had more fouls, so naturally they won. Score 5-2. 10ᵗʰ April another great struggle for supremacy took place between the Flights on the soccer field, much grovelling and cheating made for much fun and laughter."

10ᵗʰ April: Armed Recce – LINGEN area – tank, MT shot up – 1 hr 35 mins.

We had very little training in the use of the rockets, but in general I remember the technique was always to fire them in a dive and not to follow them down – an easy thing to do and the cause of a few pilot losses. Most of the targets we attacked were well defended by flak and we would usually only attack as a four-ship, and a good leader would loose his rockets and then go round to use his cannon to strafe the guns for you! If it was a large or very tough (including defences) target we would fire all the RPs in one salvo, but on Armed Recces it was more usual to fire pairs, as this gave us rockets for more than one target. We aimed using the gun-sight and the rockets usually went where you pointed them. Trains were amongst the hardest targets and we soon learnt that the safest way to attack was along the line of the train rather than broadside as the latter made it easier for any flak trucks to pick you up.

During this period I also flew 21 non-operational trips – such as Air Tests. I was a spare bod on operations, and also had practise RP firing and formation flying, and one trip to Dunsfold to collect new aircraft. It was a fine European spring – "still wizard weather with the bods sitting outside the dispersal sunning themselves" (Squadron ORB).

On the 11th of April we moved from Helmond to airfield B106 (Twenthe), still in Holland, but where we only stayed for three days. However, as soon as we landed on the 11th of April, we immediately refuelled, and off I was on operation 'No.16 Army Support Target' – Cab Rank stuff again, a German artillery HQ near Cloppenberg, which we well and truly rocketed and followed up with cannon fire: an intense and successful 55-minute foray. Later in the day I was also on another Cab Rank this time beat-up some 88mm guns at Loningen. Just 40 minutes this time but with the loss of one of our pilots.

On the 13th of April yet another Cab Rank, on which we rocketed a Hitler Youth stronghold, with intelligence estimating that there were over 1,000 in the hutted camp. The ORB recorded the op: "vectored by Wineglass to a Hitler Youth Camp; pranged in no uncertain manner, many buildings destroyed and fires started." The trip lasted 1 hr 35 mins as Helmond was now some distance away from the front-line. That was solved later in the day when 181 Squadron hopped the Rhine into Germany, taking-up residence at B112 (Rheine/Hopsten). My Typhoon was unserviceable, so rather than miss-out on this historic move, I hitched a ride with Flt Lt Ford-Coates in an Auster.

We only spent a few days at Hopsten, but in that time I flew two ops: on 15th April we set off on a Cab Rank 'do' but were recalled due to bad weather after just 20 minutes. The next day I was on an Armed Recce in the WILHELMHAVEN – BREMEN area, and in the face of masses of flak our Flight claimed two trains plus various MT and barges. This was a one-hour trip and despite the flak we all emerged virtually unscathed. That night there was an "evening feast at dispersal with a grand supper of chicken cooked over the embers of a huge fire, all washed down with an assortment of liquor. A good sing-song was held afterwards and a pleasant time was had by all" (ORB).

Next day - April 18th brought yet another move – this time to B120 (Langenhagen). During our short stay at B112 we had been based with, but not in the same Wing as, the RAF's only operational jet fighter unit, 616 Squadron, equipped with the Gloster Meteor. We called them the 'paraffin boys', because there was always a heavy smell of paraffin in the air whenever they were taking off or taxiing around.

We were soon in action again from B120: Cab Rank on 18th April to shoot-up gun pits north of Yerden on a 1 hour 15 minute trip. It was more gun-pits again the next day, South-East of Hamburg, in the face of very heavy flak, but with no significant damage to the Typhoons. Two days later the result was not so good, as Warrant Officer Calnan was shot-down, although we later heard that he was OK, but a prisoner. The target had been a group of tanks on the edge of a town and the results seemed good with most rockets in the target area.

It was at this stage that a scheme had recently been started to give one or two pilots from the Wing a week's leave in England by way of the Ansons that shuttled daily between the Wings and Croydon in London. I was one of the first to get the week's leave and I remember joining the Anson at Langenhagan en route for Croydon with a number of other pilots, mostly unknown to me. The one exception was the well-known French ace Flt Lt Pierre Clostermann DFC and Bar, a Flight Commander with the Tempest-equipped 274 Squadron. I remember having a natter with him during the flight but can't recall much of what we discussed.

The leave was soon over and upon return to B120 at the end of April, one of my friends who had joined us at Helmond, Flight Sgt Jack Steadman had met with a serious road accident, whilst out with his Flight Commander and 'Rick' Hurrell in a jeep – no doubt exploring the local German landscape. Rick Hurrell, a very well liked Australian was killed, the Flight Commander was injured and my friend Jack Steadman was very seriously injured. Although he eventually recovered, he never flew again. It was many years later in the mid 1990's that I made contact with him again by letter, and eventually by audio tape recording. Jack and his wife had been living in Kentucky USA for well over 30 years. Jack and I corresponded for over 5 years sometimes by phone until he sadly died in 2002; although I still communicate with his wife Jo.

One incident I recall whilst at Langenhagen, occurred when two of us were about to take off from the airfield. We had been delayed for sometime waiting for permission to take-off and I was getting concerned, because the mighty Sabre engine didn't like idling when waiting to take-off. It tended to oil up the plugs and could cause misfiring and lots of black smoke to come from the exhaust stacks, or even worse, the engine could die and stop. We got the green to go and my colleague got onto runway and was about to open up the throttle when he must have inadvertently pressed the gun/rocket button, for a salvo of four rockets were fired off and sailed right into the middle of Hanover. He then took off and I followed, with my Sabre engine spluttering and ejecting clouds of dense smoke from the exhaust stacks. Thankfully the engine just managed to keep going and I in turn staggered off over the rooftops of Hanover. We never heard anything about the salvo of rockets, which must have landed in the centre or outskirts of Hanover!

As the Allied advance into Germany moved rapidly, the Wing was occupying new airfields every few days, but operations continued. The Forward Air Controller directed the formation to 'something big' on 16th April, and 12 Typhoons attacked barracks at Verden near Bremen – apparently it was 'well plastered' and the following day a Hitler Youth camp near Oldenburg was destroyed.

"The Wing flew at an intensive rate for the next few days and Webb led his Squadrons on many of them. Gun positions and strong points were attacked in support of the advancing Armies and 108 sorties were flown on 26ᵗʰ April. Three days later Webb led a large formation from 137, 181 and 182 Squadrons against an enemy headquarters located 15 miles east of Hamburg. There was a large explosion and the target was left burning, sending up great columns of smoke. During April, the Wing had flown 1,231 sorties on 167 missions destroying large quantities of enemy motor transport, parked aircraft, locomotives and rolling stock for the loss of eleven pilots."

On the 1ˢᵗ of May 1945 we again moved, this time to B156 (Luneburg) and we carried out the last two operations of the war from here. Following his shooting-down and evading episode, 'Kit' North-Lewis was posted away for a rest from operations. Wing Commander G.F.H. 'Sandy' Webb DFC and Bar became our new Wing Commander Flying. A pre-War pilot, 'Sandy' Webb had flown operationally for most of the war –involved mainly with PRU work. With the war in Europe drawing to a close, he wanted one more tour of operations, and he managed to get himself appointed as Wing Commander Flying with No.124 Typhoon Wing based in Holland. He flew his first operation as No.2 of a 12 aircraft armed reconnaissance in the Steinhuder Lake area. The formation was directed to marshalling yards at Lesse and reports claimed that all the rockets hit the target. Later the same day, he led a formation and attacked two trains near Soltan. One had steam up and was carrying tanks, and in spite of 'a terrific barrage of flak' the attack was pressed home and two goods trains were left burning.

On 2ⁿᵈ May 1945 'Sandy 'Webb took-off in his Typhoon SW530 at the head of his formation on an armed recce mission. North of Lubeck he sighted a train and decided to attack it despite the presence of a flak truck. Before firing his rockets he was hit by the anti-aircraft fire and crashed in flames. He was buried by the Germans in the farm where his aircraft fell. For five years 'Sandy' Webb had led from the front. The day after his tragic death, the Typhoon Wing flew their last sorties of the

War."
Shipping Tragedy

Early May (3rd and 4th) saw the entire Wing, and indeed many other Wings, mostly Typhoons, involved over the whole two days in attacking a large force of shipping in the Kiel area. I note that my log book refers to attacking some 60 ships and I was on one Wing show each day. Very many large and small ships were attacked and many were sunk or set on fire. At our briefing we were informed that there were many Nazi fleeing the country, and we were to sink everything in sight. I well remember on Day 1 – May 3rd - a new Sgt pilot by the name of Brown, who had only just joined the Squadron, was pleading to be allowed to fly one of the (obviously) last missions of the War.

Sqn Ldr Ambrose wrote a piece for a book called 'Typhoon Attack' and included mention of this last target: "The targets did get very hot. In 1943-44 when we were flying across to France we got wary of really hot targets and tried to skirt round them, but with the war going on as it was then, a target was a target and you had to go in and cope with it. It wasn't too clever. I remember we put a piano on the back of a 3 ton lorry when we were on the move, and at the end of the war we held a service for my own 181 Squadron. On the last day of the War, I led two Typhoon Wings against a Baltic shipping convoy with the aid of a Mustang Wing led by Mike Donnet – a gallant Belgian. A chap rushed up to me and said 'could we take Sgt Brown on the op?' I asked who was he and told he had just arrived. I said 'no, we shouldn't take him on this one, this being his first operational flight. But apparently he was on bended knee to go, thinking that if he didn't get on this one, the War might end. So I relented and said 'yes', but only if his Flight Commander was happy to let him fly as No.2 to him, which he did. Sergeant Brown was the only pilot lost on that raid, so he came and vanished on virtually the very last day. When you compare that to people like myself, having done four tours on fighters and survived, you just can't beat the law of averages, which dictates that a chap gets killed on his first op while I go on forever with a charmed life. I suppose you could add about 10% skill to 90% luck. We'd lost 22 pilots from Normandy to the end, apart from chaps shot down and were prisoners, or wounded. It was very sad really."

On the 3rd of May we were airborne, led by the CO, at 1240 and ten Typhoons headed for the target area; the ORB records that: "a great mass of shipping was found forming-up NE of Kiel and eight were claimed damaged by RP; two small ships had direct hits. On the way back eight He 111s were found on a strip on the coast NE of Kiel. The CO and Flt Lt Locker-Marsh destroyed two, which were seen to burn." The second sortie, the one from which Brown failed to return, was recorded as: "the convoy was found very scattered. A direct hit with a salvo was scored on the stern of a tanker, a near miss with a salvo on a 10,000-ton vessel, and cannon attacks were made on two vessels which were already burning." On 4th May I was one of ten aircraft led by Flt Lt Garratt DFC to the same target, airborne at 1035 from Luneburg; the ORB records: "a 10,000-ton MV was attacked and left smoking South of Aro Island. An E-boat moving towards it was strafed with cannon. Three coastal vessels were hit with cannon off the coast North of Lutienburg. NW of Fehmarn Island a cargo ship of 4,000-tons was hit by RP, the ship was left smoking. Many ships were seen at Kiel and many in Fehmarn harbour."

The main comment for that day in the ORB was of a different nature: "The Great Day at last; the one that we have all been waiting for. In the evening the Group Captain announced that all animosity in Northern Germany had finished. The bar was thrown free-for-all and quite a number of people got merry." This was indeed our last operation of the War, but despite what the ORB says, somehow we all felt rather depressed and not really wanting to celebrate. The awful truth about Sgt Brown upset us all so much.

The pilots of 181 Squadron were a fine bunch and as was the case with most RAF squadrons they were a diverse bunch of characters and nationalities.

181 Squadron, No.124 Wing

Wing Commander Flying:
Wg Cdr C D 'Kit' North-Lewis DSO DFC*
Wg Cdr 'Sandy' Webb DFC*

No.181 Squadron pilots:

Sqn Ldr 'Poppa' Ambrose DFC* (Eng)
W/O Syd Ainsley (Eng) SD, safe
W/O Harry Ash (Eng)
Plt Off 'Bunny' Austin (Eng)
Plt Off Pete Ballantine (Scot)
Flt Lt 'Bergy' Bergman DFC (Dutch)
Fg Off Bob Bletcher (Eng)
F/Sgt Eric Boon (Eng)
Flt Lt Doug Brandreth DFC (Eng)
F/Sgt Brown (Eng) KIA
W/O Brian Calnan (Eng) SD, PoW
F/Sgt Nick Carter (Eng) KIA
Fg Off Chris Christian (Aus)
Fg Off Roy Cole (Eng) KIA
F/Sgt Gil Dawson (Eng)
Flt Lt 'Dizzy' Compton DFC (Eng) SD, safe
Sqn Ldt J D Derry DFC (Eng)
W/O 'Des' Desmond (Eng) SD, evaded
Flt Lt Ray Done (Eng) KIA
Flt Lt Tommy Entwistle DFC (Eng)
Flt Lt 'Freddy' Ford-Coates (USA)
Flt Lt Johnny Friedlander (Can)
Flt Lt Frankie Galbraith (Can) KIA
Plt Off Bob Gardner (Aus)
Flt Lt Bob Garratt DFC (Eng)

Flt Lt John Howard (Eng)
Plt Off Rick Hurrell (Aus) Killed in jeep accident
W/O Bill Ironside (Trinidad)
W/O 'Jerry' Jarrold (Eng)
Flt Lt 'Jenny' Jennings DFM (Eng)
F/Sgt 'Taffy' Jones (Welsh) KIA
W/O 'Kingy' King (Eng)
Flt Lt 'Lock' Locker-March (Eng)
Flt Lt Denis Luke (Eng)
Sgt A P Mann (Eng) KIA
Plt Off 'Max' Maxwell (Eng)
Flt Lt 'Mac' McGovern DFC (Aus) SD, PoW
W/O 'Doc' Milliken (Aus)
Flt Lt Johnny Martin (Welsh) Injured
Flt Lt Rod Nalder (Aus)
Fg Off 'Nobby' Noble (Eng)
Plt Off Phil Phillips (Eng)
F/Sgt 'Red' Shaw (Scot) Injured
Flt Lt Frank Sinclair (SA) KIA
F/Sgt Jack Steadman (Eng) Injured
Flt Lt Steve Stevens (Eng)
W/O Jack Vasey (Eng)

Note: KIA – Killed in Action; SD – Shot-down;
Eng-English; Aus-Australian; Can-Canadian; SA-South African; USA-American

At long last I received confirmation of my commission as a Pilot Officer – just as the War was coming to an end. The CO had informed both Warrant Officer Brian Calnan and myself, way back in March, that he had recommended us for promotion to commissioned rank, and it was in early April that Brian and I were to appear before Air Vice Marshal Harry Broadhurst, AOC 83 Group 2nd TAF for an interview. Brian was unable to attend because he was shot-down on the very day of the interview. I therefore reported to the AVM and had a quite interesting interview as he had my log books in front of him. He said he noted that I had served in the DAF (Desert Air Force) under his command and he had quite a number of questions concerning this period, and enquired about some of the Squadron Commanders. Eventually, the usual question was asked, 'why do you want a commission?' I remember, I joked saying it was not because of the uniform being of a better quality, but that, at that stage, I genuinely wanted to be able to stay in the RAF after the War and make it a career job. He seemed impressed but made no indication of whether he was going to grant the commission. It was at Luneburg on 1st May, just as I returned from a weeks leave, that my commission was approved – backdated to a date in April. So, rather late in the War – in a few days it would be over - I was told to move into the Officers Mess and get my uniform as a bright new Pilot Officer.

The War in Europe was announced as officially over on 7th May1945, and on that day we made a quick move to B158 airfield at Lubeck. This was done as a show of strength and for a few days we were all very much on edge, for the Russian Army had also moved into the German Air Force base at Lubeck. For a while it looked as if we (the Allies) would end up fighting them, but in the end we shared the same Mess with them, I now having been newly commissioned as a Pilot Officer. Lubeck had been a permanent Luftwaffe station, and I recall coming into the Mess for breakfast on the first morning – it was a very large one with many long wooden tables with chairs. I remember sitting on the same table as three Russian Officers, one a Major, when their meal was placed in front of them. Instead of eating with the knives and forks, which were laid out in front of them, they just picked up the food with their hands and pushed it into their mouths. They seemed a very uncouth, peasant-type crowd, but happily there was no trouble. I flew on 24 occasions during our stay at Lubeck, mostly formation and practise flypasts – 'showing the flag' as it were. June was taken-up with a training syllabus of dummy RP attacks, low-flying, cross-country navigation and a few exercises. There was also a heat-wave and we made good use of the beach at Travemunde.

We were at Lubeck until the Wing rotated to Copenhagen (Denmark) on 7ᵗʰ July. The visit to Copenhagen was great fun and many of the Fighter Wings were to spend a short time there. As our Wing landed I remember many hundreds of Danish people ran up to us in our aircraft, so we were obliged to hurriedly switch off our engines for fear of somebody running into our very large propeller blades. We were literally hauled out of our cockpits and whisked off to various parties and functions in Copenhagen – all a bit of a whirl. We, eventually, after about three days, managed to get a number of pilots to do a bit of flying, with mostly formation flypasts and other flying duties, until 22ⁿᵈ July, when our Squadron was selected to return to RAF Warmwell to undergo a two-week, air-to-air, and air-to-ground firing course, which most of us thought was a bit late to practise now that the war in Europe was over!

The Squadron flew to Warmwell in several stages, but because I was suffering from a heavy head cold, the Medical Officer wouldn't let me fly (as pilot), so I went along with some of the groundcrew in a transport plane. The one I selected to go in was a very large Stirling bomber that had been converted for transporting troops and some supplies. It was piloted by a Flight Sergeant and I asked him where I should sit. He recommended I sat in the nose seat where the Bomb Aimer/Air Gunner was stationed (no guns now). The position was literally right at the very nose of the aircraft, and apart from the superb view from the front I was able to look back to the pilot's compartment. We had an uneventful trip to Warmwell, but on arrival, I noticed that the airfield was just a small grass field, and I remember our pilot remarking over the intercom that he didn't think he would be able to get into such a small field, but that he would try. Remember, I was the guy, yards in front of the landing gear and the rest of the aircraft! Anyway, he made a goodish landing and we finished up with the wheels almost touching the boundary hedge, but I was high up and well over the hedge in my isolated position in the front gunner's seat! However, all was well (no damage) and the Stirling was pulled back and round so we could taxi to the control tower area.

As I previously mentioned, I was not allowed to fly Typhoons because of my head cold, and the possibility of affecting or damaging my ear-drums when the aircraft was in a dive, but on 4th August I was asked (told!) to take a Fg Off Lesson as passenger to London and return (by myself) in a Miles Martinet. The flight was uneventful, but because I didn't have all the maps needed I had to go down low to find out where we were – this I managed to do by reading the names of railway stations (now put back after the end of the War). My passenger just wanted to get to London and didn't mind where, so I eventually found an airfield, which I discovered was RAF Leavesden. I had no R/T so wasn't able to call up the control tower, so I just landed and taxied to the opposite side of the airfield from the control tower and told Lesson that this was the nearest I could get to London! He started to grumble, but I soon shut him up – because I wanted to get away before being really noticed, and him knowing where he was!

On my return to Warmwell, the CO asked me what I'd done and said I should have reported to the control tower. Anyway, that was that, and I never heard any more about it. Another one I seemed to have gotten away with!

On the 5th of August the Squadron returned to Copenhagen and I returned (because of the head cold) by transport plane. We stayed at Copenhagen until September; thoroughly enjoying every minute of our stay. In all, I flew some 16 flights during the spell at Copenhagen – all practice cross-country exercises. The Wing left Copenhagen on 18th September and landed at our new base at Schleswig (B164) in Germany, and where we were now referred to as No.121 Wing. We were only there for just over a week, for on 27th September the Wing returned to the UK, to RAF Dunsfold, for the very sad purpose of disbanding. I flew my last trip in Typhoon IB MN756 (E) on the 3-hour transit flight, with one stop to refuel. I remember landing at Dunsfold and watching our beloved Typhoons being 'pushed' or towed off the runway into nearby fields where I understand they were to be scrapped. The Squadron was officially disbanded on 30th September 1945; for most of us a very sad day.

After spending a day or so collecting our passes we were all sent on leave to await further instruction as to our next posting – remember that it would take some time to reach 'demob' day.

'Poppa' Ambrose had left us during the last spell at Lubeck, and I remember him coming into the Mess just after the War in Europe had ended and proudly saying he had volunteered the Squadron for service in the Far East (Tiger Force). I can't say we were over pleased to hear this, but of course the war ended on 15th August 1945 (VJ Day). We said good-bye to a fine CO and pilot, a great character, and one we looked up to.

Anyway, it was very many years later (early 1980's) I noticed an ad in an aeroplane magazine mentioning a certain book soon to be published, which included a contribution from Wg Cdr 'Poppa' Ambrose. I sent a letter to him via the magazine and one evening, well over 20 years ago now, I answered the telephone at home and the voice said, 'Hello – it's Poppa Ambrose calling!' Well, we had a very long and extremely interesting talk. He said he had stayed in the RAF after World War Two and became a Wing Commander, flying jets until he retired. At the time of the phone call he was a Director of a well-known travel company. He invited me to call on him at his home near Farnborough but I never went, however, I certainly valued the phone call from our old 'Boss'.

The day we left Dunsfold to go on leave was something I shall always remember. After a hectic party in the Officers Mess, I awoke with a rather a thick head, along with most of 181 and 182 squadron pilots, and we travelled by truck to Godalming railway station to catch a slow-running local steam train to Victoria. I was with one of my pals and we selected a carriage, which was already occupied by two rather elderly ladies sitting opposite each other in the compartment of the non-corridor train to London. There was lots of rowdy noise as the pilots from the two (now disbanded) Squadrons were cramming into various carriages along the train. After quite a while the train got underway. We hadn't been going for very long before it juddered to a halt and the guard was seen walking along the track shouting 'I'm not moving the train until you all get off the roof and the outside of carriages'. A lot of the guys were clambering about on the outside of the train, so they all got back into the carriages and we started moving again.

181 Squadron: February 1945-September 1945

Period	Aircraft	Main Airfield
3 Feb-11 Apr 1945	Typhoon IB	B86 Helmond
11-13 Apr 1945	Typhoon IB	B106 Twenthe
13-18 Apr 1945	Typhoon IB	B112 Hopsten
18 Apr-1 May 1945	Typhoon IB	B120 Langenhagen
1-7 May 1945	Typhoon IB	B156 Luneburg
7 May-7 Jul 1945	Typhoon IB	B158 Lubeck
7-21 Jul 1945	Typhoon IB	B160 Kastrup
21 Jul-4 Aug 1945	Typhoon IB	Warmwell
4 Aug-6 Sep 1945	Typhoon IB	B160 Kastrup (Note 1)
6-9 Sep 1945	Typhoon IB	B166 Flensburg (Note 1)
9-27 Sep 1945	Typhoon IB	B164 Schleswig
27-30 Sep 1945	Typhoon IB	Dunsfold - disband

Notes:
1. Jerry records the departure from Kastrup as 18th September.
2. Dates used here are based on Squadron official movement records.

But, not long afterwards, there was a tap on the outside of one of our windows and we lowered it. It was one of 182 Squadron pilots simply asking if anyone had got a bottle opener to open their bottles of beer. It amused us as the two elderly ladies started to go through their bags looking for bottle openers. 'No' they said, they had no openers, so along to the next carriage, on the outside, went our 182 pilot, until once again the guard stopped the train until he returned to his carriage, then off the train went yet again! The train was stopped once or twice more until we got to Victoria. As my pal and I got off at Victoria and started to walk along the platform, a large crowd of our Squadron pilots were running along the platform carrying a huge stuffed stag head with large antlers, which had been taken off the walls of the

Officers Mess, which was a rather large old country house where we were billeted at Dunsfold, and the whole crowd were being led by my old Flight Commander, now CO of 182 Squadron, John Derry. The last I ever saw of good old J.D, as we all called him, was he with his merry men, and the giant stags head, disappearing down the Underground escalator. I often wonder what happened on the tube train and to the stags head!

A brief stay with 695 Squadron

After a couple of weeks at home on leave, I received a telegram posting me to RAF Lasham to attend a course as an Air Traffic Controller. I'm afraid I wasn't very happy with this and I immediately got on to someone I happened to know who was involved in posting of operational pilots, asking him to do something to get me onto a flying job to see me out until my demob day. He said 'take no notice' of the Lasham instructions and he would try and get me a flying post. So, strings having been pulled, it was in late November that I was posted to 695 Squadron based at Horsham St Faith (now Norwich Airport). The Squadron had moved to Horsham from nearby Bircham Newton in August 1945, taking with it a very diverse fleet of aircraft that were used in the Anti-Aircraft Co-operation role.

No.695 Squadron (split into two flights) was a target-towing and fighter affiliation outfit co-operating with Army and Navy guns. We had Spitfire XVI and a few old Vultee Vengeance IV aircraft – the Spitfire for Army co-operation and fighter affiliation and the wretched Vengeance for target towing. I started my short spell flying with 695 Squadron with two flights on the 29th of January 1946 both on Spitfire XVIs – two Sector recces. A 30 minute solo on the machine was quite hairy – especially coming into land – for in my anxiety to get down in one piece I was inadvertently using the foot brake (I'd only ever been used to the other forms of braking) far too heavily immediately I touched down and <u>almost</u> tipped the wretched thing on its nose.

The rest of my flying was in Spitfire XVI (a further eight times), and each involved flying as target practise off shore for the Army/Navy people near by – no live ammo.

The last time I flew an aircraft in the RAF – or anywhere for that matter – was a Spitfire XVI, on 8th March 1946, just one day after my 24th birthday. It was a beautiful day and I had one hour and five minutes of local flying and aerobatics. What a way to finish!! I had intended applying to stay in the RAF but a short taste of the peace-time Air Force persuaded me not to. I stayed with 695 Squadron until 9th April 1946, when I was told to proceed to No.100 PDC at RAF Uxbridge where I was released from the RAF the following day. In all I flew just 800 hours, including two tours of operations, but, after almost six years in uniform I was a civilian again. There was a mess-up with my pay and indeed my promotion to the exalted rank of F/O (Flying Officer). The reason for the mess-up was undoubtedly because I had ignored the Lasham posting. I eventually got my back pay and Flying Officer status.

And so my war was over. I had encountered sadness and a little fun, I had been scared, I had been lucky, but to answer the question posed by the title of this book ……..I survived the War!

REMEMBERING THE PAST

There has only been one of my wartime colleagues who I have regularly kept in touch with: ex W/O Syd Ainsley – whom I met and became friendly with during our service in 181 Squadron. Syd, who lived in Rugby, and I, met quite regularly for a number of years, and he would drive down to stay at my home on many a weekend. I also met up again with my pre-war friend Dennis Porter, who had served as a Wellington pilot during the war years. He, Syd and I would spend the weekend together enjoying football at Leyton Orient, and then going on to see ice hockey at Wembley. It was Dennis who introduced me to my future wife, Audrey, who was the daughter of the licensee at The Wake Arms pub in Epping Forest. After a couple of years, these meetings fell away and in 1952 I married Audrey and saw very little of Dennis again, but with Syd I've always kept in touch.

It was my wife's efforts that kept much of my Air Force memorabilia intact including my uniform, helmet, log books, and many photographs, newspaper clippings, and letters. I was, of course, interested in aviation and the RAF in particular, but never bothered much in keeping it in order. After the untimely death of Audrey in 1990, I had met up with my friends Jean and Roy Cane and they helped me considerably in those awful dark days. They encouraged me to interest myself in joining the Typhoon and Tempest Association, which met annually at Shoreham Airport. I have been able to attend most years, with Jean accompanying me at the event while Roy takes care of their three small 'doggies'. It was at one of these reunions that I met our old Wingco Flying, now a retired Air Commodore 'Kit' North-Lewis DSO, DFC and Bar. I also became a member of 80 Squadron past members who arrange an annual reunion each March, since the Squadron disbanded in September 1969. I keep in touch, but have only attended one reunion, which is held in the RAF Club in London. There was no-one of my era there, as they were mostly post war air crews. The Squadron had converted to Canberra aircraft, and unfortunately I found I had nothing much in common, as most of the war time people had either passed on or were too frail to attend.

It was just a few years ago that, after noticing an advert in one of the aircraft magazines, Jean encouraged me to reply. It was from a Brian Calnan who was trying to get in touch with old colleagues of his in 257 and 181 Squadrons, and in particular for Sqn Ldr Ambrose to contact him, or any of the other pilots who he knew. Well, I remember Brian of course, because he and I were both due to attend an interview with the AOC (Broadhurst) regarding our commission – unfortunately it was the very day that Brian was shot-down and badly wounded and taken POW. Jean persuaded me to write, which I did, and I received quite a nice letter from Brian who was living in America. He said that he really wanted to look up our old CO, 'Poppa' Ambrose, mainly because they were both Sergeants together in 137 Squadron. He went on to say that he had received a letter from a friend of 'Poppa's', a Group Captain, who informed him that 'Poppa' had just recently died. Brian said he had recovered from his bad injuries, had married and had been living in California for many years. He said he wouldn't write again, but I might like to know that another one of our fellow pilots, F/Sgt Jack (John) Steadman was looking to contact any of his colleagues from 181 Squadron, and gave me his address, also in the USA, in Kentucky. I wrote to Jack and we corresponded by audio-cassette for 4-5 years before he died; I still keep in touch with his Welsh wife Jo. Last year with Jean's help I arranged for a small plaque to be placed, and a rose tree planted in the small garden of Remembrance at Shoreham. Jack's plaque happens to be right next to one in remembrance of our wartime AOC, Air Chief Marshal Sir Harry Broadhurst. Also remembered in the small area are many past members of Typhoon and Tempest Squadrons, including the late Sqn Ldr John Derry. Incidentally, information from Ken Rimmel earlier in 2003 said that they were unable to continue with the Museum at Shoreham, and that the June reunion would be taking place at a farm near Chichester.

Sqn Ldr Ambrose's article in 'Typhoon Attack' also mentioned the fate of Brian Calnan: "I was able to piece together what happened to Brian Calnan. Brian and I had been great friends since our time in 257 Squadron together. Later when I got a Squadron I had him posted to it. I put him up for a commission but the day he was due to see the AOC Harry Broadhurst, he was shot down near Hamburg and we thought he'd been killed as no-one saw him get out. I'd thought I'd lost a good friend, wrote to his parents and had his gear sent to them. Then, at Luneberg Heath in May 1945, just before we left to go to Lubeck, I got a message to go out to a Dakota on the airfield. When I got to it I found Calnan in plaster from his neck downwards, both arms broken. He looked at me and grinned - 'Do you see that WAAF Boss?' and I said 'Yes'. 'Well, if she thinks she's safe with me going back across the English Channel, she's well mistaken!' I could have hugged him – that is morale!"

Other information that has only recently come to my attention concerned my first CO, Sqn Ldr R.E. Bary DFC, when I joined 80 Squadron at Bu Amud in January 1943. According to the book 'A Clasp for the Few' (New Zealanders with the Battle of Britain Clasp), Ron Bary applied for an RAF short service commission in 1938. His application was successful, and he sailed from New Zealand for the United Kingdom in the RMS 'RANGITATA' on 16th December 1938, and was eventually posted to 229 Squadron later in October 1939 as an Acting Pilot Officer. In May 1941, now a Flying Officer, he was posted to the Middle East, attached to 73 and 274 Squadrons in the Western Desert. In October 1941, now a Flight Lieutenant, he was appointed Flight Commander to 250 Squadron, and on 23rd January 1943 took command of 80 Squadron at Bu Amud in Libya (a couple of weeks after I had arrived). Sqn Ldr Bary was with us until mid June when he left to command No.239 Kittyhawk Wing as Wing Commander. Whilst he was with 80 Squadron we converted from Hurricanes to Spitfires, and I note in my log book that I was taken up in a Harvard piloted by Ron Bary prior to my going solo in Spitfires. Wg Cdr R. Bary continued to lead No.239 Wing into Sicily and from airfields in Italy until January 1944, when he was tour-expired and returned to UK, attending the Central

Fighter Establishment at Millfield.

Shortly after Christmas 1944 he was posted overseas for his third operational tour – to become Wing Commander Flying, No.244 Wing, operating Spitfire fighter-bombers in North Italy. On 12ᵗʰ April 1945, Bary took off with two Spitfires of 92 Squadron to make a close-support bombing attack on a target north-east of Imola. After reaching his objective, Bary dived to drop his two 500 lb bombs. At an altitude of 4–5,000 ft his aircraft was seen to explode and disintegrate. There was no flak, no enemy aircraft were seen, and it was assumed that, when the bombs were released, a faulty fuse detonated and caused the explosion. Another, but remote possibility was small arms fire from the ground. Bary's body was recovered and buried in the British Empire Cemetery at Faenza. In February 1946 an award of the DSO (to add to his DFC) was made, with effect from the day prior to his death. The citation described Ron Bary as an outstanding Wing Leader, who gained the absolute confidence of all pilots under his command.

On my one and only visit to a 80 Squadron Reunion at the RAF Club in Piccadilly, London, which I attended in March 1995, I was rather disappointed to find no-one was there who served during my (almost) two year spell with the Squadron. However, there was one old boy who was a pilot with the Squadron in, and prior to, the Greek campaign, who asked me what I thought of the Gladiator performance against the Hurricane! At the dinner table, I sat opposite someone who was the Squadrons' last Adjutant. He did finally speak to me after I had been introduced as a World War Two pilot with the Squadron, flying Hurricanes and Spitfires. I remember him introducing himself and saying, 'you were one of the OR's (Other Ranks) – I was indeed a NCO pilot at the time. During his time, all the aircrew were apparently officers. I wasn't very impressed!!

As I left, the chap who runs the reunion said that a researcher had contacted him the day before, and he was trying to find out about a Spitfire, which was on the Squadron at the time I was there, and had been donated by the people of Edmonton in North

London. He was in the process of researching details of who flew it, and so on. He asked me if I remembered ever flying the 'Edmonton' Spitfire. – I didn't know, but I said that I would ring the researcher, which I did next day – a Peter Saunders – who was pleased to get my call, and he asked me if I'd flown the 'Edmonton' Spitfire. I said I had no idea, as we really didn't bother to find out who made a donation on a particular aircraft. When I asked him if he had the official number of the aircraft, he said he had and gave it to me. It was Spitfire Mk IX MA845. I looked in my log book, and low and behold, I had flown this particular aircraft on two occasions – once on 6th June 1944, on D-Day over the Normandy Beachhead landings, and again on 8th June, again over the Beachhead. At this news he was now very excited and wanted more details.

We exchanged two or three letters and I called in with my friend at Leiston, an old wartime airfield where US Mustangs operated, and where he is now involved with a caravan site. He wasn't there, and I've heard no more from him! He did send me some copies of Squadron Record Book obtained from the Public Records Office detailing the pilots name, aircraft number, date, time in and out, and Report and details of the various missions; actually it was quite interesting stuff, and it had a lot more detail of each operation than in my own log books. Another one of our 80 Squadron colleagues that I was re-united with in the mid nineties was Warrant Officer Hugh Ross, who joined us at 80 Squadron, just as we disembarked from Naples, Italy, in April 1944 to return to the UK, and he remained a close friend until I was made tour-expired at West Malling near Maidstone in Kent in late August 1944. Hugh went on to operate with 80 Squadron at Manston and on into Europe with the Tempest Wing, but, while at Manston, Hugh and Flt Lt Johnny Heap took-off on the 14th of September for the Hague with the task being to look for and note any enemy movement inland of the Hague – this was in preparation for the Arnhem Operation. They finished off their recce by attacking a large white boat or barge with 20 mm cannon, and shortly after pulling away, Hugh noticed his oil pressure starting to drop; they both set course for home, until it became obvious that he would not make it back to England. It was either bale out now while over land, or force-land in Holland – both options resulting in becoming a PoW. The other option was to get as far out to sea as possible, bale out and hope the parachute and dinghy worked alright and that air/sea rescue would pick him up. Hugh decided to take his chance in the North Sea. He has been rescued from the sea once before in the middle of the Atlantic when the troopship *Anselm* was torpedoed and sank with the loss of 300 lives, (about 700 including Hugh were picked up). Hugh baled out of his Tempest in mid North Sea when his engine finally stopped and managed to get into his dinghy. F/L Heap was watching overhead and had radioed for help. Two Spitfires quickly came, and soon afterwards Hugh was picked up by Walrus and taken back to England.

Whilst I only had one quick trip in the Tempest, I was impressed with the aircraft, and it seems that 80 Squadron, and others, found it an excellent machine for this period of the war. In 'Spud' Spurdles book 'The Blue Arena', he had this to say: "Every now and then Hun aircraft were found by our Tempests and hopelessly outclassed, we clobbered them; only the Me 262 jet fighter-bomber was faster. It was considered such a threat with its lightning bombing attacks on our 'dromes (mostly with anti-personnel bombs) that standing instructions were that when one was sighted, it had to be reported in clear on the R/T. Immediately every free-ranging fighter converged on the nearest known 262 base and hung around in case one flew in to refuel. With their short range and special ground servicing requirements, the jets were vulnerable on coming in to land at their known haunts. The Huns created flak 'corridors' along which the returning 262's would fly at treetop height. It was extremely dangerous to attack them but our chaps, excited by the challenge of bagging a 262, took fearful chances braving the concentrated fire of dozens of multiple flak guns. In this way one of 80's pilots, a quiet unassuming chap, Warrant Officer H.F. Ross strafed and killed Major Walter Nowotny, one of Germany's leading aces. There have been many versions and claims for the encounter but, Ross saw this 262 taxiing near some hangers on the Rheine runway and, ignoring the intense flak, dived to strafe. The Enemy aircraft ran into some trees and the pilot was killed.' Hugh and I still exchange phone calls – he lives in Middlesbrough – and a few years back, I was able to meet him in London, and we both took a trip to Hendon Air Museum for lunch and a very good natter.

Shortly after my leaving the RAF in 1946 and returning to civilian life, I was looking forward to seeing my father again. Apart from seeing him in 1940 when he and my mother saw me off from St Pancras Station when I joined the RAF, and the one other time I saw him during the war years, Christmas 1945, I cannot remember seeing him again until in late 1947. He decided that it was time to retire from the Merchant Navy at the age of 57, and in February 1948 he finally retired, but first decided to undergo a routine operation for hernia – on the Company as it were – at the Seaman's Hospital at Greenwich. All seemed to go well, but on 19th February, my mother and I were called back to the hospital, as my father had developed complications and was on the danger list. We stayed overnight at the hospital, but sadly Dad died during the night at the early age of 58. It was a shattering blow for my dear mother and myself; gone were all the hopes of getting to know him better and to be able to discuss his career in both World Wars, and gone was the opportunity for him to enjoy all those hard earned years of peace after the War. Dad was deservedly awarded an OBE for his services during World War Two, and I'm very happy to recall that after much research for dates and details, I finally found the official Citation signed by the King – complete with the citation for the award - and the OBE itself.

I have great admiration for members of the Merchant Navy, and, in particular I am very proud indeed of my father, serving first in World War One as a junior engineer, and through the peace years and into the Second World War, when he was an experienced Chief Engineer. I do so wish I could have got to know him better.

My dear mother was now (February 1948) left on her own, for I was to marry in 1952. My wife and I were always near at hand, and kept an eye on her and took her out until she finally passed away at the age of 87 in 1977 – almost thirty years after my father died. I'm afraid that she always had a rather lonely life, as I was an only child, and my father having being away from home for extended periods.

I was recently reminded of a TV programme shown on the History Channel called 'Typhoons' Last Storm', and I rather naturally assumed it would be something to do with 'rough' weather conditions. But no, it was an hour-long program (including the usual boring advertising breaks), which depicted the very last operation that Hawker Typhoon fighters took part in over the two days of 3rd and 4th May 1945. On referring to my Log Books I confirmed that I had taken part in the operation on each of the two days. The 3rd of May was referred to in my Log Book as a Shipping Strike – Kiel Bay – 1 hr 10 mins – with remarks noted as 'Wing Show on 60 ships, and then on the 4th of May, again Shipping Strike – KIEL BAY – 1 hr 45 mins – Remarks 3,000-tonner damaged. It was on the 3rd of May that we lost Brown on his first op. as related previously. I recall the briefing for this operation, which was described as a large number of Hitler Youth and troops, including high-ranking SS Officers fleeing Germany to set up resistance elsewhere, possibly Norway; our orders were to destroy as many ships as possible. Typhoons from various Wings, plus others, including Mustangs and Mosquitoes, duly pounded these ships in relays from dawn to dusk over two days. Apart from the sad loss of Brown on his first operation, and, incidentally, the loss of our new Wing Leader, 'Sandy' Webb the day before, it had left us all in a unhappy mood, and we didn't feel too inclined to celebrate the end of the War in Europe on the 7th of May.

We were based at B156 Luneberg in Germany where we operated on these final two days, but on the 7th May we moved to Lubeck to face up to the Russians, who had started to occupy the German airfield at Lubeck, so the attack on shipping in Kiel Bay was almost forgotten. However, I was reminded when reading that most important book by Norman Franks, called 'Typhoon Attack', when I referred to the entry by our CO of 181 Squadron at the time, Sqn Ldr Ambrose. In the book he mentions the last days of the War in Europe saying that he led TWO Typhoon Wings against a Baltic shipping convoy, with the aid of a Mustang Wing led by Mike Donnet. He then goes on to describe the loss of F/Sgt Brown, but with no further details of the actual operation.

Well, I was horrified to learn from the film that the last shipping strike had a terrible ending. It appears that, following the mass break-through and impending end to the war in Europe, the wretched German Higher Command was now very worried that the Allies would soon over-run a number of the infamous slave and mass extermination camps that existed in the Lubeck area. The Allies had already come across the totally disgusting Belsen and Buchenwald Camps, and it would seem the German High Command did not want the free world to find all these other similar camps. So, they sent out a message to all their camp commanders to evacuate all the living prisoners and transport them by cattle trucks to the seaport of Neurnstad for loading them (many tens of thousands) onto ships, and then the SS secret service released messages on the underground network, knowing that the British Secret Service would pick them up. The messages were, that large numbers of German troops and Hitler Youth, including senior high-ranking SS and Nazi Officers, were about to embark and sail to Norway to resume the fight; the Germans knowing full well that British Intelligence would order the bombing and complete destruction of all these ships and the many thousands of these displaced persons – which of course, tragically, the RAF did. The film shows some shots of Typhoons attacking the shipping with bombs, rockets and of course cannon fire. Several pilots (now elderly) from 197 and 184 Squadrons are shown in the film discussing the operation, and all, of course, had no idea of the slaughter we were creating. I must say, after all these years, I felt deeply upset that I was part to blame for the tragic occasion.

Epilogue - May 2005

On the 20th of April 2005 – I was lucky enough to be offered a flight in a light single engine aircraft – a Piper Cherokee Arrow PA28 G-AWAZ, owned by my Doctor, Paul Manders. I immediately accepted his offer, and the next day, the 21st of April 2005, with Paul at the controls (dual) and myself sitting by his side (there being two further seats behind us), we took off from Elmsett, Suffolk (a small grass airfield) just south of RAF Wattisham. We set course for the Detling beacon and on to West Malling, circling both the old RAF aerodrome at Detling (grass), and West Malling (concrete runway), before setting off back across the Thames to seek out where the old RAF base at Hornchurch was situated – sadly its now a built up residential area. We then found our way to the old RAF station at North Weald where we landed, and spent a short time relaxing in the sun before taking off for the return flight to Elmsett.

Shortly after takeoff, Paul told me to take over, and I was delighted to be able to fly the plane for almost 10 minutes between Chelmsford, and Colchester, soon handing back the control to Paul. We flew over my house in Lawford and enjoyed the rest of the flight over Manningtree and Hadleigh and then back to Elmsett. A truly delightful trip for me, and on one of the best days for flying of the year, with beautiful clear blue skies, no clouds, and just a fair wind. This flight almost happened to coincide with the time of year when I was serving in 80 Squadron, which had recently (April 1944) returned from the Middle East theatre. Three Squadrons (80, 229, and 274) were then recalled to the UK to be part of the Invasion of Europe force leading to, and taking part in, the D Day landings. On 5th May 1944 our three Squadrons reformed at RAF Hornchurch with Spitfire IXs and spent a very short time there working up as a three-Squadron Wing (to be known as the Detling Wing) under Wing Commander 'Hawkeye' Wells, moving to Detling on 20th May 1944 and starting operations the next day. My involvement that day was being part of a Wing sweep over France, and later on that day I was also included in practise Squadron formation flying.

We operated from Detling from the 21ˢᵗ of May on a daily basis with Wing sweep, top cover to Bostons, sweep and Ramrod, Scramble to intercept 15+ bandits over Hastings, and Beachhead patrols over the D Day landings until 23ʳᵈ June, when we moved to Tangmere sector and on to Merston – a Tangmere satellite station. Not staying there very long (just over 7 days) we then moved on to RAF Gatwick – again moving to West Malling on the 5ᵗʰ of July. There were more escorts, sweeps and Ramrods, and target cover for Halifax and Lancs. I finished my tour with 80 Squadron at West Malling on 11ᵗʰ August 1944.

Imagine my extreme pleasure at being able to over-fly Detling nearly 61 years and one month later and being able to look down and locate the actual RAF aerodrome; just a field then on the ridge just north of Maidstone and now a green corn field. There is no flying now, of course, but from just 2,000 ft I was sure I could see myself, and some of my fellow pilots, coming into land from a fighter sweep operation over France, seeing just a few huts, and landing on that same green field. I was able to re-see it all. A truly superb and moving experience – one of which I will remember for the rest of my days!!

APPENDIX A: RECORD OF SERVICE

Dates	Location	Unit	Country
26 Jul 1940-1 Aug 1940	Cardington	Receiving Wing	UK
1 Aug 1940-22 Aug 1940	Bridgenorth	Drill Centre	UK
22 Aug 1940-10 Jan 1941	Pembroke Dock	210 Sqn	UK
11 Jan 1941-13 Feb 1941	Yatesbury	Radio School	UK
14 Feb 1941-18 May 1941	Castle Rock	Radar Station	UK
19 May 1941-24 May 1941	Stratford on Avon	ACRC	UK
25 May 1941-9 Jul 1941	Cambridge	No.2 ITW	UK
16 Jul 1941-30 Aug 1941	Peterborough	No.32 EFTS	UK
11 Sep 1941-28 Feb 1942	Montrose	No.8 SFTS	UK
17 Mar 1942-29 Apr 1942	Usworth	No.55 OTU	UK
29 Apr 1942-13 May 1942	Annan	No.55 OTU	UK
21 May 1942-30 May 1942	Wilmslow	PDC	UK
24 Jun 1942-4 Jul 1942	Takoradi	Transit to ME	West Africa
9 Jul 1942-7 Sep 1942	Almaza	No.22 PDC	Egypt
7 Sep 1942-19 Sep 1942	El Ballah	No.1 METS	Egypt
19 Sep 1942-17 Oct 1942	Almaza	No.22 PDC	Egypt
17 Oct 1942-27 Oct 1942	ADU HQ	ADU	Egypt
27 Oct 1942-1 Nov 1942	Almaza	No.22 PDC	Egypt
1 Nov 1942-4 Nov 1942	Wadi Natrun	No.25 PDC	Egypt
4 Nov 1942-16 Nov 1942	LG203	No.1 RSU	Egypt
16 Nov 1942-23 Nov 1942	Sidi Heneish	No.1 RSU	Egypt
23 Nov 1942-26 Nov 1942	Tmimi	No.1 RSU	Egypt
26 Nov 1942-9 Jan 1943	Gazala	No. 1 RSU	Libya
9 Jan 1943-15 May 1943	Bu Amud	80 Sqn	Libya
15 May 1943-5 Jul 1943	Idku	80 Sqn	Egypt
5 Jul 1943-11 Aug 1943	Savoia	80 Sqn	Libya
11 Aug 1943-29 Aug 1943	St Jean	80 Sqn	Palestine
1 Sep 1943-5 Sep 1943	Derna	80 Sqn	Libya
5 Sep 1943-12 Sep 1943	Bu Amud	80 Sqn	Libya
12 Sep 1943-16 Sep 1943	Derna	80 Sqn	Libya
19 Sep 1943-17 Oct 1943	El Ballah	MECGS	Egypt

22 Oct 1943-9 Nov 1943	Savoia	80 Sqn	Libya
9 Nov 1943-19 Nov 1943	Kabrit	80 Sqn	Egypt
19 Nov 1943-13 Dec 1943	Heliopolis	80 Sqn	Egypt
13 Dec 1943-3 Feb 1944	Kabrit	80 Sqn	Egypt
3 Feb 1944-22 Feb 1944	Madna	80 Sqn	Italy
22 Feb 1944-13 Mar 1944	Canne	80 Sqn	Italy
13 Mar 1944-4 Apr 1944	Trigno	80 Sqn	Italy
4 Apr 1944-25 Apr 1944	Naples	80 Sqn	Italy
25 Apr 1944-5 May 1944	Sawbridgeworth	80 Sqn	UK
5 May 1944-19 May 1944	Hornchurch	80 Sqn	UK
19 May 1944-23 Jun 1944	Detling	80 Sqn	UK
23 Jun 1944-28 Jun 1944	Merston	80 Sqn	UK
28 Jun 1944-6 Jul 1944	Gatwick	80 Sqn	UK
6 Jul 1944-23 Aug 1944	West Malling	80 Sqn	UK
1 Sep 1944-13 Oct 1944	Bicester	No.13 OTU	UK
13 Oct 1944-1 Jan 1945	Harwell	No.13 OTU	UK
2 Jan 1945-7 Jan 1945	Tangmere	No.83 GSU	UK
7 Jan 1945-25 Feb 1945	Dunsfold	No.83 GSU	UK
28 Feb 1945-11 Apr 1945	Helmond	181 Sqn	Holland
11 Apr 1945-13 Apr 1945	Enschede	181 Sqn	Holland
13 Apr 1945-17 Apr 1945	Rheine	181 Sqn	Germany
17 Apr 1945-1 May 1945	Hanover	181 Sqn	Germany
1 May 1945-7 May 1945	Luneburg	181 Sqn	Germany
7 May 1945-6 Jul 1945	Lubeck	181 Sqn	Germany
6 Jul 1945-22 Jul 1945	Copenhagen	181 Sqn	Denmark
22 Jul 1945-5 Aug 1945	Warmwell	181 Sqn	UK
5 Aug 1945-18 Sep 1945	Copenhagen	181 Sqn	Denmark
18 Sep 1945-27 Sep 1945	Schleswig	181 Sqn	Germany
27 Sep 1945-22 Oct 1945	Dunsfold	181 Sqn	UK
22 Oct 1945-20 Nov 1945	Lasham	No.84 Gp DC	UK
20 Nov 1945-9 Apr 1946	Horsham St Faith	695 Sqn	UK
10 Apr 1946-4 Jul 1946	Uxbridge	No.100 PDC	UK

APPENDIX B: AERODROMES LANDED AT

UK
Annan
Bicester
Cranfield
Detling
Dunsfold
Edzell
Finmere
Gatwick
Grantham
Grove
Harwell
Hatfield
Hornchurch
Horsham St Faith
Leavesden
Merston
Montrose
Moreton Valence
Ouston
Peterborough
Stracathro
Tangmere
Usworth
Warmwell
West Malling
Weston Zoyland
Woodley

ITALY/SICILY
Canne
Catania
Madna
Trigno

MIDDLE EAST
Aboukir
Abu Sueir
Benina
Bu Amud
Daba
Derna
El Adem
El Ballah
El Firdan
Gambut
Gazala
Heliopolis
Idku
Kabrit
Martuba
Mersa Matruh
Savoia
Sidi Barrani
Sidi Heneish
St Jean
Tmimi
Wadi El Natrun

NW EUROPE
Copenhagen
Enschede
Gilze-Rijen
Helmond
Langenhagen
Lubeck
Luneberg
Rheine
Schleswig

APPENDIX C: AIRCRAFT FLOWN

DH Tiger Moth	52 hours
Miles Master I, II, III	80 hours
Hawker Hurricane I, II, IIA, IIB, IIC	205 hours
North American Harvard II	4 hours
Supermarine Spitfire VC, IX, XVI	346 hours
Hawker Tempest V	1 hour
Vultee Vengeance	2 hours
Hawker Typhoon	110 hours
TOTAL 800 hours	

APPENDIX D: LETTERS FROM COLLEAGUES

1318229 W/O P.L. Godfrey,
80 Sqdn.
R.A.F. Manston,
Nr. Ramsgate,
Kent.

5.9.44.

Dear Jerry,

Many thanks for your letter. I certainly am sorry to see that you have both landed for such a bloody awful stooge job. It sounds really awful, and I must certainly keep out of the way of anything like it. Joe went up to Stanmore a couple of days ago, but as yet have heard no news of him. I told him where you and Stan had gone, so he said that he would try for the same place, but you know what the R.A.F. are like!

I certainly am missing both of you. This place is certainly ideal for a good pissy life. We all were on the booze the first few nights, but it has quietened down just lately, thank goodness. Anyway this place is the gen.

Actually the N.C.Os are living in Westgate, away from the camp, which is a good thing! We sleep in a private house on the seafront and the Mess itself is about three hundred yards away, also in a private house. It really is a wizard spot, the grub is tops and served up attractively too. Of course having civvy cooks does make a great deal of difference. There is not much beer in, but that doesn't matter, for the pubs are quite close.

As for the time off racket, well that is really good. One day off one on, and very little doing then, certainly gives me plenty of scope. Of course practice flying does interfere but not *very* often. We are nearly finished with doodlebugs now, as you can guess from the news. Nobody has got one, and very few ever see any. I don't know what we shall be on next, but you and S. have a pretty good idea.

There are quite a few trains up to London but the journey takes a bloody long while. Usually three hours. Still if you and Stan can get down here we can easily put you up and have a good pissy together. Talking about beer, as I have said we got cracking the first few days, and 'B' Flt. got together one of them. It was a grand party with plenty to drink. Some old dear of about 65 looked in and danced "Knees up Mother Brown". Johnny Heap joined her, it was a great joke. The C.O. was there and started talking to a WAAF, so Dobbin piped up with "You'd better be careful of him he will try and seduce you" in his usual quiet tones! Much consternation among the blue bloods but we all thought it was a great joke!

Incidentally I hope to be having eight days leave from Oct. 6th, so you and Stan must come up to London, and we will have a day together.

Well that must do for now. Tell Stan not to get tight on too many occasions or else he'll be drinking me under the table. Take care of yourselves, and Happy Landings, or should I say "TOWINGS"!

Your old Pal
Peter

> 1169221 W.O. Horsey, H
> 80 Squadron, B.L.A.
> 17.10.44.

Dear Jerry,

A letter arrived for Pete Godfrey from you and I took the liberty of opening it to get your address.

Unfortunately the squadron has been through a very bad patch and amongst our losses was poor old Pete. He went in just off the Dutch coast about a month ago and I am afraid there is no hope of his survival.

In ten days we lost six of the boys and two more baled out but returned safely. First we had Jock bale out in the Channel, he was picked up safely and was back with us in a couple of days. Then we lost Spike who may be a prisoner and Ullestad was injured. The following morning Pete went and Paddy Irish baled out over the 'drome in the evening. To follow up Lofty Haw was killed the following morning and Bob Hanney vanished on the way back. A week later Willie Wiltshire and Willie Williams did not return, but Williams called up to say that he was hitting the silk. We hope they are both O.K. A few days later the squadron was sent overseas and now we are rotting away in Holland. 274 are with us with Johnny Heap as C.O. and Johnny Halford back complete with D.F.C. They lost Wilkes a few days back.

Life here is very dull, no night life of any kind and the beer in the mess not worth drinking. Our average bed time is 8.30. During the day when we are not flying our time is spent building a dispersal hut. The bods are all rushing round with tools in their hands banging in the odd nail when the C.O. is about. He has appointed himself chief slave-driver and it is impossible to dodge him for more than five minutes. We may finish it by Winter next year.

The only other news is that the Yanks phoned a few days ago to say that Dutchy has been killed. Tough luck eh! The boys send their best wishes and wish to be remembered to Stan.

> Cheerio for now.
> All the best,
> Harry.

1169221 W.O.Horsey,
80 Sqdn.
18.11.44.

Dear Jerry,

I'm only a month late answering your letter so I don't suppose you have moved yet. We are still in the same dump and still have a few old faces on the squadron. Andy left us a week back - tour ex. and Paddy and Murray Adams finish next week. But we still have Spud, Tony, Judy, the Hussies, Jock Findlay, Haggis and yours truly to keep the old squadron going. Johnny Heap is still going strong with 274 but since losing Wilkes they have lost Cole. Bill Weir is back with them, with two fresh holes in his legs. It seems to be their turn for bad luck.

Since we have been here our spare time has been spent building a dispersal and the completed article is quite a work of art. It had three rooms the "Chute House", "Der Feuhrer's Orifice" and the pilots' room, consisting of brick fireplace, card section, bar and works of art from Men Only. The whole joint is named "Spud's Speakeasy" and is easily the best building on the 'drome. Of course we had a party to open it - any excuse - and a good time was had by all. Beer, whiskey, gin, brandy, vermouth and champagne were amongst the offerings. Some people passed out for some unknown reason but I managed to face it until the bar was dry. I don't think the Group Captain and myself were quite sober, - I was calling him ' cobber and he was calling me 'sir' - but we were at least on our feet.

I had a letter from Les a while back, he hopes to be back in England soon. Maybe you will both come back to the squadron. By the way, I am on leave from Nov. 28th until Dec. 6th, so if you are in town you can ring me, Thornton Heath 2793 is the number. The boys send their best wishes and Jock says he may write to you some time. Don't forget to write and perhaps we can meet while I am at home. Remember me to Joe when you write.

Cheerio for now.
All the best,

Harry.

APPENDIX E: THE DEATH OF FLYING OFICER HARRY HORSEY

From the start of his operational flying in Malta in June 1941 to his death in April 1945 Harry Horsey had flown 850 operational hours. He was an Old Boy of Selhurst Grammar School and a quote from one his letters is included in the School's Book of Remembrance:

"Some months after leaving Malta I went on to the Middle East: Syria first then the Western Desert where I was to spend 15 long months chasing Jerry and being chased; long months broken only by two short spells in Cairo. During this period I advanced with Ritchie to Benghazi, and back to Gazala. Then followed the great retreat to Alamein. Another advance with Montgomery's ground effort which unfortunately I left at Derna. In the blue I flew practically every single-engine aircraft from the ancient Vincent and Lysander to the more modern Hurricane. "Out of the fighting area I converted to Spitfires and ferried them on the long route from the Gold Coast, West Africa, via Kenya to Cairo. It is the most amazing trip, stretching across miles of swampy territory to flat colorful sandy areas; across mountains, more sand, and up the green skirted Nile to our base. The whole trip took several days, and it is with relief that one first sights the pyramids, and knows that another aircraft has almost reached the Middle East. More important to us – a bath, a few beers, and a few days comfort await us in Cairo before returning to the white man's graveyard.

"My next posting was back to Italy for more operational flying, but with the help of a forced landing, which kept me for a short time in hospital, I managed to visit North Africa and spend six weeks resting. Now I have returned to Italy, and a spot of revision before returning to a squadron, the RAF insists I stay here for another tour."

The Air Ministry announced the murder of Fg Off Horsey: "On April 2nd, 1945, made a forced landing near Boesel in Oldenburg, and was taken in for the night by the local Burgermaster, who informed the nearby aerodrome of his presence. At 10 a.m. on the following day two German airmen escorted him as a prisoner of war back to Varrelbusch aerodrome, but on the road they treacherously shot him in the back of the neck. He was buried in the cemetery of St Celias's Church, Boesel, Oldenburg, by the parish priest."

The two German airmen were arraigned for trail on 21 January 1946 charged with "committing a war crime in that at Boesel, Germany on the 3rd April 1945 in violation of the laws and usages of war were concerned in the killing of Flying Officer Harry A Horsey, RAF prisoner of war."

The trial took place over three days (21-23 January) and both men pleaded Not Guilty. The following are extracts from the proceedings of the military court; as the authors of this book have not seen the complete proceedings we have remove the names of the two airmen:

"The airman having been brought down the previous day was taken by soldiers to the house of the Burgomaster at Boesel, and remained in the house that night sleeping in a sitting room with only an old man – unarmed – to guard him. The next morning the two accused, who were Feldwebel, arrived on bicycles to take over the prisoner and escort him on his way to PoW camp. They had two cycles with them, one (airman) was armed with a machine pistol.

"After the party had proceeded some distance by road without incident, (one airman) having experienced some difficulty in managing the two cycles and an anti-tank rifle given to him by the local Burgomaster to hand into military HQ, stopped at a farm to try and get some rope to secure the rifle. It was arranged between him and (Airman B) that he should follow up, (Airman B) went on with F/O Horsey, walking immediately behind him with a machine pistol, in the ready position under his arm. Before (Airman A) could rejoin him, (Airman B) had shot the prisoner. There were passers-by on the road during the journey. No-one apparently witnessed the shooting.

"On 25 October a British pathologist examined the airman's body and gave clear evidence that there were two bullet wounds, one in the back of the neck fired at very close range, which must have proved immediately fatal, another through the back at an angle which may well have been fired at a body already on the ground. "Having shot the airman, (Airman B) showed considerable agitation and phoned almost at once to report the fact. He said that the airman wanted to attack me or to defend himself. When questioned he gave two successive accounts, both circumstantial, one with diagrams, describing how, when following the airman the latter made a quick movement, which if not intended to get rid of his escort at least was sufficient to alarm him as to his intentions, and that in the excitement he fired a short burst from his machine pistol. He was, he said, at the moment just completing the lighting of a cigarette, with the machine pistol still under his arm. It was urged in further excuse that he had suffered from severe concussion, and was nervous, excitable and even unstable.

"(Airman B's) statement was not consistent with the pathologist's evidence. On the other hand it was confidently asserted in evidence that the machine pistol was incapable of firing single shots, and the only witness who heard the shots fired – a girl – formed the impression that the shots were in quick succession.

"It may be that the fatal wound as described by the pathologist is typical of this kind of war crime. That all the evidence of F/O Horsey's behaviour and of the circumstances with a number of passers-by make it unlikely that he would choose that moment to try and escape. No official enquiry into the death of a PoW was held, as was usual.

"In fairness to (Airman B) it may be added that evidence was given that it was his regular duty to escort captured airmen and that of his treatment of them had hitherto been correct.

"(Airman B) was sentenced to life and (Airman A) was acquitted."